# Dedication

To the River of Life

and the Great Adventure

of the Journey to the Sea.

# Lessons from the Sessions

## Reflections of Journeys in CranioSacral Therapy

Don Ash, P.T.

*Lessons from the Sessions*
Don Ash
www.DonAshPT.com

ISBN 0-9766523-3-1

Printed in the United States of America
Third Printing, June 2006

# Contents

# Acknowledgements

I gratefully acknowledge and wish to thank:

My wife Jill for allowing, encouraging, and supporting my personal growth.

My daughter Sarah and son Doni for providing me the privilege, challenge, and honor to be a parent.

Helen Buchanan (Huron South Dakota) for teaching me to always be a patient advocate, to learn my anatomy, and to laugh at myself.

John Upledger for supporting me and providing me with the adventure of a lifetime and teaching me the importance of listening to the wisdom of the body. It has been his bravery and unyielding faith in the work that allows us to be here talking and working in this space called CranioSacral Therapy. He has truly shown us the road to promoting health and wellness. He continues to call us all gently, but emphatically, to be agents in making the World a touch better.

Gloria Ash and Dorothy Hannigan for teaching me loving kindness and allowing me to be their witness.

Mary Anne Balser for her skill and patience in the daunting role of "Don's typist."

Sibyl Meade for her editing talents.

The wonderful staff of Odyssey Press of Gonic, NH, for their skill in giving birth to my first book. I thank you all

And finally to my patients, (my teachers) who have allowed me to be a part of their very personal growth, change, and healing.

# About these Sessions

*I*n order to present these experiences in detail, it is important to me that the sacredness of the session is expressed as accurately as possible. It is also of the utmost importance to ensure the privacy of that sacredness. It is in this spirit that names, genders, and certain happenstance may be altered slightly to maintain privacy and confidentiality. All the experiences of these sessions are related to the methods taught by Dr. John Upledger, D.O. O.M.M.

For more information about CranioSacral Therapy and a complete listing of seminars, references, research, and books, go to www.Upledger.com.

Or write to:

Upledger Institute
11211 Prosperity Farms Rd.
Palm Beach Gardens, Florida 33410-3487
Tel: 800-233-5880

# Foreword

*A*s I reflect about the reasons for writing this book, I am reminded of the concepts of A.T. Still. Particularly—structure follows function. He looked at human structure and tried to understand what function it served in the body. It was a unique way of looking at the body because it was simplistic and based on common sense. And it awakened the idea of wholeness in looking at ourselves— to view the body as a unit and the potential for self-healing as a whole person.

This little book is about using structure to understand content and function. Since the middle of the 19th century there has been a growing movement in healthcare that embraces the concept that structure begets function. At the center of A.T. Still's work is the river of life, the cerebrospinal fluid. In the mid 20th century from Sutherland, and in the latter 20th century and to date by way of Upledger, the work continues.

Sutherland nurtured an understanding of structure and Upledger nurtured an understanding of function in a marriage of traditions that gave birth to CranioSacral Therapy (CST). It has been a difficult marriage because of the politics of medicine and territories of healthcare professionals.

I am a physical therapist doing CranioSacral Therapy. I think it is ultimate physical therapy, but I have found after years of working and teaching the subject, that the truth of the matter becomes simpler and simpler. I am a P.T. doing P.T. I am a P.T. doing CST. I am a manual therapist doing gentle manual therapy. I am one person working on another person. I am one person witnessing another person healing themselves. Here are two souls awakening the potentials of their bioenergetic organic units. This book is about that; the structure and function of that.

The structure of the contents of the book is to first define what CST is. My hope is that my definition is simple enough for lay people to understand, and a working model of what I actually say in the first session with my patients. Other essays here move the reader through the structure and beauty of the body. We then see the work in the context of our culture with things I've learned about the current hospital-based medical model, insurance, pain and suffering. Then I take you through experiences I have had with my patients in my travels—so that at the end of each essay there is a statement of a lesson I have learned—and maybe insights we can both use. As you move through the book I think you will see we move from structure and anatomy to elements of SomatoEmotional Release, visualization and dialogue.

These are essays of experiences and lessons taught to me, most generously, by people in a state of dynamic change. I record them in honor of these teachers. My hope is to inspire the reader to the potentials of life experience via CranioSacral Therapy. You are most welcome to take what truth you find and leave the rest. Central themes repeat but I hope I made the book thick enough to be read by more than the parakeets.

# Introduction

/t is rather seldom that an author allows the reader to see exactly who he (the author) is, what he does, who he was, and what he used to do—as well as how he made the transition from then to now. In this book Don Ash has shared it all with you. There are no secrets. Don used to be a conventional physical therapist. He followed all of the rules of that profession.

In June 1988 Don Ash began his transition when he took the Level I CranioSacral Therapy class presented by The Upledger Institute. During this class Don was introduced to the craniosacral system. This is a rather new physiological system that was first discovered by William Sutherland, D.O., in the early 1900s and which was confirmed at Michigan State University by a research team in the Biomechanics Department, led by yours truly. During this introductory CranioSacral Therapy class Don not only learned of this newly recognized system intellectually, he also learned to feel its activities with his own hands on another person's body. He also learned to use his hands to therapeutically affect this craniosacral system using a very light touch, equal to about 5 grams—the weight of a nickel.

As things progressed in the class Don became acquainted with the major influences that the craniosacral system has on all of the other systems, tissues, and fluids of the body. Its influences range from skull to tailbone and from the core between skull and tailbone to finger tips and toes of the body. During the class Don saw and felt through his hands the craniosacral system's effects upon the brain and spinal cord, as well as the meningeal membrane system that encases these structures. He also learned about the influences the craniosacral system has upon the spinal nerve roots; the sympathetic and parasympathetic divisions of the autonomic nervous system; and the very important balance that is maintained between these two divisions of the autonomic nervous system. Don also became acquainted, through his hands and brain, with the strong influences that the craniosacral system has upon all of the glands of the body and especially the master gland (pituitary) and its connection with the hypothalamus structure of the brain, which has so much to do with emotional states and stresses and how they manifest via the pituitary gland to the other glands of the body that comprise the endocrine system. Don Ash was formally and irrevocably introduced to a physiological system that, although poorly recognized by conventional scientific and medical wisdom, he knew existed. He had felt it with his own hands. He could feel this system's activities and effects. He trusted his hands to tell his brain what was happening.

Two months later Don took the second level CranioSacral Therapy class. During this class he fell totally in love with Cranio-Sacral Therapy, its concepts, and its applications. He came to know that he could and would help suffering people with his hands as the only instruments, as he "blended" energetically with the patient. In January 1990 Don completed the CranioSacral Therapy workshop curriculum with the Advanced class. He also completed special workshops in CranioSacral Therapy which specialized in brain dialoguing and the dissection of fresh cadavers. These cadavers are not embalmed and not usually frozen before being studied and palpated by the craniosacral students.

I am very pleased to let you know that Don Ash has become one of the Upledger Institute's outstanding teachers in Cranio-Sacral Therapy and Dissection classes.

Regarding this book, Don Ash shares with the reader many of his journaled observations, thoughts, experiences, and learnings. Don also shares descriptions of his errors and how his conscience affected him when he did err, or just plain did not know what to do. Don shares his feelings as he learns to "blend" and follow the patient's bodily wisdom. He lets you know that there are no boundaries that are not set by either the therapist or the patient—or sometimes both. Don describes how he was led to understand that he is a facilitator. He follows the advice of the patient's inner wisdom. He subordinates his own thoughts to that inner wisdom. This switch to a facilitator is sometimes difficult. Old habits often die hard. Don has effectively made this switch. He is a true facilitator. He "blends" in order to discover what the patient's body requires in order to heal, then Don follows instructions from the patient's inner wisdom. Don Ash has learned that death can be a wonderful transition rather than a fearful event. He has excellent descriptions of the death transition in this book.

Don Ash is a very generous teacher. In this book he shares much that has happened during his transition from conventional physical therapist to facilitator of self-healing by the patient.

Don, thank you for sharing.

John E. Upledger, D.O., O.M.M.
Palm Beach Gardens, Florida

# Part I

# CST and the System Defined

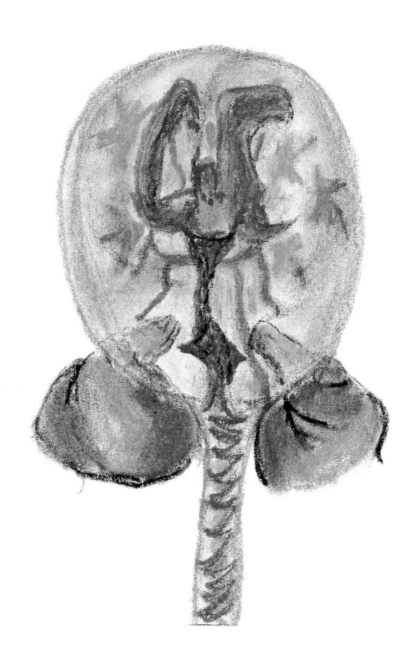

# 1

# What is It?

As I travel around the country teaching I find the most frequently asked question is:

How do I first explain CranioSacral Therapy (CST) to my patients who have never heard of it before? I am a massage therapist, how do I tell someone I also do CST?

Tell your patients, "Hey I've learned a new technique that may help you in addition to our regular (massage, PT, OT, Chiropractic, etc.) session. Would you like to try it?"

The patient may ask, "Well, what is it?" My lesson from many sessions is in the frequent times patients have asked me to explain, prompting me to create the explanation I'll share with you now.

This is what I tell them: "Everyone has several kinds of rhythms in their body. There is the cardiac rhythm, in which the heart beats 60–80 times per minute. Then there is the respiratory rhythm of your breathing, in which you inhale and exhale 15–20 times per minute. Underneath those rhythms is another one called the CranioSacral Rhythm (CSR). In this rhythm your head gently expands and narrows and your spine gently lengthens and shortens in an effort to exchange and circulate cerebrospinal fluid. It does this 6–12 cycles per minute. The membranes that surround your head and spine act as a little hydraulic pump that draws this clear fluid out of your blood, bathes the brain and spinal cord with it, and then returns it to the blood supply. In this way the cerebrospinal fluid is filtered and renewed. It is important fluid because it supplies nutrients, carries away waste products, and acts as a fluid protective covering for the brain and spinal cord."

"The cardiac rhythm can be felt at the neck, wrist, and ankles. The rhythm of the lungs can be felt at the shoulders, neck, chest, and belly. Like these other rhythms, the CranioSacral Rhythm can be felt from all over the body—the legs, pelvis, sacrum, shoulders and head."

"If I were to hold your ribs and resist your lungs from expanding, you would move to allow your lungs freedom to continue their rhythm. What we do in CranioSacral Therapy is *very gently* hold the rhythm and watch as the body gently moves to free itself. As it does this, releases occur and restrictions in the body change. Just as bruised ribs from a fall might keep you from breathing properly, a fall on your tailbone or a bump on the head may keep your beautiful craniosacral system from working properly."

"So we gently hold and wait for releases. Releases occur in the form of heat, pulsing, muscle twitching. Sometimes the eyes may blink or gurgling sounds occur in the digestive system. You may feel part of your body soften, or gently shift and spread. Breathing patterns may change. A deep feeling of relaxation is a common reaction to treatment."

Some releases are gentle, but sudden. I offer this analogy as an example: "Have you ever come home from a hard day and said to yourself, oh boy, am I tired, I can't wait to go to sleep tonight? So you get into your bed, the room is dark, and the house is quite; you can feel sleep overcoming you. Your eyes get heavy and just start to close—and surprise!!!!!! Your body jumps. Has that ever happened to you?" Ninety-eight percent of patients nod their head yes to this. I continue, "The other thing that can sometimes happen with this work is that your body may get very still before or during the release process. It's a special point because it is a Significance Detector for your body. Sometimes as your body is resting here on the air mattress and my hands are listening to the rhythm of your craniosacral system, your body might move into the position it was in when you got hurt. This often happens with people having pain and dysfunction from slips, falls, motor vehicle accidents, and traumatic events such as being beaten up in a fight. Your rhythm automatically stops, and releases begin to occur. You enter a point of stillness we call a significance detector because the position the body moves into, or what you are thinking, is often an important (significant) part of the healing and letting go process."

Sometimes there are emotions held in the body that are a part of the release process. I once had a patient who could not remember what had happened after being in a single-car accident. She was a single mother caring for two young children. She was in a lot of pain, unhappy, and concerned because her pain and limited range of motion in her neck and arms had gone on for over a year. She was fearful she would be unable to continue to care for her children.

She had been to conventional therapies such as PT, OT, Chiropractic, and had been seen by orthopedists and neurologists. Nothing seemed to help.

When she came to me I explained to her about CranioSacral Therapy, and the cranial rhythm. I also told her about releases and allowing the body to release what it will. I asked her to lie down on her back and I began to listen to her rhythm at her feet, then her thighs, then her pelvis. At the pelvic diaphragm, she gently turned and curled up into the fetal position, closed her eyes, and said her ankles, wrists, shoulders, and neck hurt. She said she could see the color red. She then began to cry. Her rhythm had stopped.

I kept my hands in the pelvic diaphragm position, with the patient still on her side. I told her these were emotional and physical memories held in her body that were releasing and if she could stay with this process for a few minutes it would be helpful. She was able to stay with the process for five or six minutes and then she stopped crying, straightened out on the table and sat up.

She said, "You know, now I can remember the accident." She explained in detail that she didn't see the black ice and she felt the car start to skid. "I saw the telephone pole coming towards me and I tried to press hard on the pedals, my feet went under the pedals. I straightened my arms out with a strong grip on the steering wheel and I remember being so scared and thinking about who would care for my children and what would happen to them. When the crash came I felt pain in my ankles, wrists, and shoulders. I felt my neck snap and the last thing I saw just before I blacked out was the red hood of my car crashing through the windshield."

She then tried to turn her neck and exclaimed, "Wow, I can turn my neck and I don't have pain. What just happened?" I explained about still points and Significance Detectors. That is to say, her body moved into the position it needed, in order to release the effects of the trauma from the motor vehicle accident. It also provided her with a SomatoEmotional Release (SER), releasing an emotional charge that accompanied the trauma at the moment of impact and immediately after.

She came in twice after that session for massage and exercise, and then I discharged her to return to family life pain free.

So, CranioSacral Therapy is a gentle method of listening to the body and encouraging change. It is using very light touch (5 grams) to encourage releases that may include heat, pulsing, gurgling of the digestive tract, muscle movements, and breath change. Releases may be emotional, in the form of tears, laughter, and/or memories—that may produce feelings of fear, shame, sadness, anger, remorse—that also can come to the patient's awareness and thereby release.

The most important part about CST, and a real lesson from every session, is that the body will lead the way, and do what the patient needs—and do what the therapist is able to help facilitate. Therefore, massage therapists, PTs, OTs—those practitioners who want to work with the physical body—will do that (facilitate), and experience, by and large, all physical releases, (heat, pulsing, etc). Those therapists who feel confident in assisting with emotional release usually invest a lot of time and energy training in SomatoEmotional Release and may facilitate that event for the patient. The body is able to recognize the level of work the therapist is able to facilitate.

After a short discussion with the patient covering some of the elements I've mentioned, I ask if it sounds like something they would like to try. They usually say yes and away we go on our adventure.

# 2

# Founders

Where did this work called CranioSacral Therapy come from? Interestingly enough CST has only been broadly introduced to the public as a therapeutic modality for about 20 years through the Upledger Institute. But its roots go back over one hundred years.

One reference has it that Andrew Taylor Still, a Civil War colonel, while suffering a headache, decided to lie down, resting his head on a fallen tree trunk. His headache vanished and he realized specific physical pressure could relieve pain. Still became a physician by apprenticing with his father who was a physician and had a practice in the state of Missouri in in the mid 1800s.

Dr. A.T. Still began his practice in 1854. He had a wife and three children. In 1864 they all came down with meningitis. In those days it was known as the flux. The treatment at the time was a dose of arsenic. His family was given the treatment and three members died. His biography states that what then followed was a dark 10 years. He spent much of his time alone.

He emerged from that time with the conviction that drugs were bad, the body could heal itself, structure followed function, and the physician was to view the patient as a whole person and not just a bad leg or sore back. He went on to prescribe exercise, and develop manual techniques of manipulating the bones of the body to ensure alignment and clear nerve pathways. He founded Osteopathy and the school of Osteopathy at Kirksville Missouri in 1892. The methods that he began developing in 1874 were for manipulation of the bones. One of Still's students was Palmer, who felt more aggressive manipulative techniques were most effective. They disagreed, parted ways, and Palmer then went on to develop Chiropractic medicine.

Another one of Still's students was William Garner Sutherland who attended Kirksville around the turn of the century (1898). Sutherland was a lover of anatomy and intrigued by Still's admonition that structure follows function.

Sutherland was infatuated by the joints of the skull and postulated that joints are for movement and therefore movement must be occurring in the head. He was most intrigued by the temperoparietal sutures and how they resembled the gills of a fish. What possible reason could there be for movement of the bones that composed the skull, he wondered.

He began experiments on himself. He used linen bandages, baseball mitts, a football helmet, and several common household materials that he placed around his head at different times in attempts to limit movement. He then employed his wife to keep a journal of any behavior changes that might occur. One reference records Sutherland placing a wooden butter bowl on his head with screw plates at strategic locations, alternately screwed down to immobilize different parts of the skull. So in the whole scheme of things, one of the true pioneers in this work is Mrs. Sutherland because she had to live with this "Scientist."

What this wonderfully innovative anatomist and his wife found was that he exhibited problems with balance and gait stability. He had vision problems, speech and vocabulary difficulties. He had back pain, neck pain, and headaches. He had many common symptoms of the day that he saw in his patients. History has it that he placed a piece of rug on his office wall and knocked his head against it to try to free the joints of the head he had artificially immobilized. He quickly recognized this was likely a treatment approach that would not be financially rewarding and had inherent risks. So he began using light, sustained touch upon the head in an effort to squeeze the fluids of the head (particularly—cerebrospinal fluid) around to the restricted joint to help open it from the inside out. This process is much like squeezing a small package of two crackers in order to burst open the plastic seam at the package end.

Sutherland went on to found the school of thought called Cranial Osteopathy. I place this date to coincide with the publishing of his first book on the subject called The Cranial Bowl in 1939. He wrote in medical periodicals under the pen name of Blunt Bone Bill. He endured harsh criticism and consternation from the osteopathic community, but did have a loyal group of followers who advanced the work within the exclusive domain of Osteopathic Medicine.

John Erwin Upledger attended Kirksville in the mid 1960s. He wanted to be a physician who performed surgery and prescribed medications. He had very little interest in holistic medicine back then. In 1971 he was assisting a neurosurgeon in the removal of calcific plaque from the cervical spine, when an event happened. After opening a hole in a cervical vertebral lamina, both doctors observed a rhythmic movement of the dural membrane in and out of the hole they had created. Unable to explain the event at the time, Upledger researched and was eventually referred to Sutherland's work in cranial rhythmic impulse and the holistic health benefits of circulating cerebrospinal fluid. He began studying Sutherland's work and became an accomplished cranial osteopath, which led him to Michigan State University's Bioresearch Department at the school of Osteopathy. He was part of a group of 22 researchers and clinicians that had been given a grant to prove or disprove Sutherland's theories of cranial bone movement. Upledger and a couple of other researchers implanted electrodes on the heads of monkeys and put radio signals through them. The least little change in the distance between the (antennae-looking) electrodes would make a recordable disturbance in the radio wave. This proved without a doubt that primate skull bones move. He also developed an anatomical model to explain circulation and the production/reabsorption cycle of cerebrospinal fluid called the Pressurestat Model. Probably the major contribution of Upledger was that he established the mind body connection of SomatoEmotional Release as a tissue release trait of the body. His early work involved performing CST on autistic children. Frequently they would have an emotional outburst and then have dramatic shifts in decreased symptoms. Balance, eye/hand coordination, attention spans, and tactile defensiveness changed for the better. Most notably his teaching encouraged the intentional stoppage of the cranial rhythm by the therapist. This event causes the body to release restrictions that had been preventing good health. Therapists are trained to recognize these releases which can be physical, emotional, or energetic.

His later work involved dialoging with specific organs, tissues and cells to resolve restrictions that inhibited the body's natural healing process. This dialoging brought the micro consciousness to the awareness of the consciousness of the whole patient, unifying and maximizing the patient's healing potential. This work was fundamental in the Upledger Institute-sponsored programs to help Post Traumatic Stress Disorder with Vietnam Vets—releasing war trauma—and the Compassionate Touch Program, stemming violence in schools. He also introduced and promoted the use of intentionally directed energy to promote health. He introduced the model of energy cyst, that is, an area of high energy embedded into the body from external environmental force associated with trauma. By placing hands on the body and directing energy, this excessive energy can be dissipated and tissues can return to normal health and function.

He also promoted the fundamental concepts that the body is a unit and can heal itself. Both notions were original concepts of

Still, but Upledger developed them into the concept of the Inner Physician. His emphasis is that if we touch the body very lightly and listen, the body will tell us or show us where to go to effect change for the patient.

And finally, no one in either the 19th or 20th century has introduced this light touch work to more people than Upledger. As of 2004 the Upledger Institute has had over 70,000 people attend seminars that are offered 400 to 500 times per year around the world. His book, co-authored by Jon Uredevoogd, *CranioSacral Therapy* remains a classic in the field. He has authored eight books on his vision of CranioSacral Therapy. Moving gentle cranial work out of the realm of Osteopathy, making it accessible to a variety of body workers, has caused great angst and anger from the osteopathic community and isolated Upledger from his profession. He is not bothered by that.

I have been blessed to have had Dr. John Upledger as my teacher, mentor and friend. We recently had breakfast together in Montreal and he told me stories about Still and Sutherland.

As he relates it, one time the osteopathic students had a beer party at the old clinic on the hill at Kirksville after hours (circa 1960). It was after exams and everyone was just letting go of the stress of exam time. It was in the early morning that an old African American man came by and found these young lads in the basement talking and having their last beer. Each introduced themselves and the man said he had been the carriage driver for A.T. Still.

With the encouragement of these young osteopathic students the old man began to tell them stories of the old days. He said all these founders were temperamental and difficult to get along with. Palmer couldn't get along with Still, so he split. Still thought Sutherland was crazy, so he split. That caused Sutherland to go off and develop Cranial Osteopathy and Palmer to develop Chiropractic.

It's ironic that Upledger couldn't get along with his Osteopathic community so he split and founded the Upledger Institute. Sometimes personal difficulties lead to positive change.

The carriage driver said Still was very cantankerous. Still would ride a horse and have him follow in the horse carriage. Still would ride out in the country and knock on the doors of farmhouses, asking if there were any sick inside. He carried an old knobby wooden cane he used to wrap on the doors, so it was a very loud knock. If there were someone ill, Still would treat them in the front room of the home. If further treatment were required he would load them in the carriage and bring them back to the clinic. That's how he got patients in the old days. He would also go to the train station and meet the trains. Passengers would get off the train complaining of back pain from the prolonged sitting. He would treat them right there by pressing the knob of his wooden cane in their backs. If they weren't better, he'd load them in the carriage and bring them back to the clinic.

Both Still and Sutherland dug up graves to study bodies. Still found that the most degenerative organs of each cadaver had a shrunken or disrupted blood and nerve supply. He then devised a manual technique to liberate the joint of the spine corresponding to the nerve that went to the degenerated organ. That's how Osteopathy was founded. Sutherland found that most of the skulls had available movement in the temperoparietal suture (the joint just above the ear). He would pry at them with his pocket-knife. That's how Cranial Osteopathy was founded. So Still brought the notion that the body heals itself and spinal manipulation liberates the pathways of the nerves of the organs. Sutherland advanced the idea that cranial bones move. Upledger molded these thoughts with energy, emotional release, and the inner wisdom of the body to bring us to today and CST.

Essentially none of these men invented anything, they just found it again. Chinese physicians have listened to the rhythm in the body for four thousand years. The Paracus culture in Peru (2000 BC to 200 AD) practiced cranial molding. Hippocrates, the Greek physician, is known to have used traction to reduce lumbar disc problems. Christian priests practiced "laying on of hands." Native Americans molded infant heads with papoose cradles. Shiatsu has incorporated cranial work, visualization and moving energy for well over 100 years. Many cultures of antiquity had bonesetters. In the Renaissance Age in Europe, both Michelangelo and De Vinci felt that cerebrospinal fluid was important in nurturing intellect and the soul. Both felt the seat of the soul was in the large open fluid vessels of the lateral ventricles.

The most important aspect about these founders and a lesson for me is that they all have enormous respect for the human body. They all are lovers of anatomy and the exquisite design of the structure and function of these marvelous vessels. And they all have the conviction that the human body, every body, has within it the capacity to heal and change. They also all have a certain reverence for life and know full well that we are all mortal. To each there is a season. Irrigated fields grow and prosper when fluids move. When seeds are planted with intention and cultivated with awareness, honor, and respect they will bear fruit.

# 3

# *Beauty*

*W*hen we have a CranioSacral Therapy Dissection class, it is a special event because it is one of the few opportunities in the world for manual therapists to feel real human tissue intact in an unembalmed human cadaver.

The study of the human body in its natural state, without formaldehyde, is not allowed in Great Britain or Spain. Physicians and other healthcare practitioners must travel to the U.S. and then only in a precious few settings are people allowed to feel the tensions within the tissues of the body without preservatives.

As we hold a dissection class I have several requirements for participants. First, they are to relax and recognize they are on a great adventure of discovery. Then they are to remember that they are completing the last wishes of this body that is before them. The person, who is now our cadaver, elected and arranged for their last act to have their body taken apart and studied. Due to circumstances, luck, karma, and the way of the world and beyond, we have been charged to complete that last request. That said, there comes a responsibility to look and feel, and to study the structure, texture, and interrelationships the tissues and organs have together, in forming a human being. We, as participants in this last event of organized disassembly of this body, need to complete the task with respect, honor, courtesy, compassion and sharing. We need to look deep, feel each structure and contemplate how this body moved through a lifetime. What did she think, what did she do? How does function relate to structure? How does this body work as a unit? Is there any spirit or energy left compared to an embalmed cadaver? Can we feel tension in the falx by placing gentle pressure on the sacrum? How strong, flexible and elastic are the cranial membranes, the dural tube, the lungs, heart and liver? How much or how little manual traction is required on the cranial bones to effect a palpable change in the falx? All these secrets and lessons, wonders with answers— surprises; are before us if we only open our eyes and minds, and look deeply and feel authentically.

Three days in the lab fly by. Hours are moments and only recognized by a sense of fatigue at the end of the morning and at the end of the day. Students come with personal observation goals. Some have had visceral or knee surgery, and they want to look at the gallbladder or medial meniscus. Some wonder what it would be like to hold another person's heart, eyes, or brain. Some want to look at the arachnoid and the trabeculae. Others want to see where the sphenoid connects to the occiput at the synchondrosis. Still others want to see cerebrospinal fluid in the dural tube. What does the inside look like at the knee, ankle, elbow, or hand? What do the jaw joint and the disc look like, and can we move the jaw and see the disc move?

Being the leader of the group, I jot down these requests for exploration. As we open the class after an introductory meeting and orientation to the lab and dissection procedures, I have all of us circle the dissection table and hold hands. I offer a moment of respect and gratitude for the real teachers of the class, the cadavers.

As the three days unfold, we actually bond to the cadavers in gratitude for allowing us to look into their bodies. Commonly, the students offer up their assumptions of the cadaver's life as a living being. We give the main cadaver a name. It might be Mr.

Ferguson or Nelly, or some other name that endears us to this generous former living person.

On my last dissection class, one student was so moved as to bring in a CD from a Canadian Country Folk singer. She read us the words of the song. The following day another student brought in a small portable CD player and we played the song in our morning group meeting on day 3. Here are the words: (written by Laura Smith)

### Beauty

My legs, they are a part of my body
My eyes, they are a part of my soul

Look deep, Look deep,
There's a surprise there,
There's a surprise there,
Such a surprise

I'm a Beauty

My feet, they are the tools of my traveling
My hands, they are the tools of my trade

Touch deep, Touch deep
There's a surprise there,
There's a surprise there,
Such a surprise

I'm a Beauty

My face, it's a map of my time here
My heart it's a map of my dreams

Dream deep, Dream deep
There's a surprise there
There's a surprise there

Such a surprise, Such a surprise

I'm a Beauty.

We found our cadaver had bilateral lens implants in her eyes, ovarian cyst, ovarian cancer, a polysystic single kidney and osteophytes on the right femoral condyles. She also had a sub-arachnoid hematoma in the frontal lobe of her brain. It was in this class—with all that we saw and felt and learned—that we decided to name her Beauty. Lesson from the session here is that the body is beautiful and holds wonderful secrets. When we do CranioSacral Therapy, we need to look, listen, and touch deep with our hands, for there is always a surprise there, such a surprise. Each exploration is a gift and an adventure.

* *Beauty suffered pneumonia and dropped her body in her 89th year. Her pastime in the winter of her years was spent, in part, operating a loom.*

Thank you Beauty!

# 4

# Clinical Applications of the Dissection Experience

Whenever I tell family and friends what I do now, they say, "What? You mean you actually cut somebody up? You like that?? Why would you do that?" Seeing the expression of disbelief on the faces of enough people I know gave me pause, and I asked myself, "You like dissection? Why is that?"

So, during the last dissection class I paused several times and asked myself why I was there and was I sure this was something I wanted to continue to do. As I watched the students and their wide-eyed wonder and awe at the sight of the brain, the membranes, and other significant structures, answers began to flood my consciousness.

First and foremost, I have always been struck by the magnanimous gift of these humans who volunteer to donate their bodies. I mean, here they are, lying here intentionally, as their last earthly act. They have willed their bodies to be turned over to others unconditionally. As a matter of fact, the only condition they are assured of is that they will be dead and their earthly vessel will be taken apart. There is a tremendous implied intimacy in the fact that they are trusting us with their bodies unconditionally and without pretense. There is no makeup, no clothes, props, or setting—other than a high stainless steel table in a cold, well lighted room.

The dissection class is an anatomy class. It is an observation class. But more than anything, it is a palpation class. I remember as a young person working with clay, I could see what shape I wanted to create with the clay, but until I felt the soft texture, the flexibility ranges with strength and weakness extremes, I couldn't use it. To see and then also to feel at the same time enables me to instill these characteristics of the tissues of the body into my tactile discrimination and the palpatory abilities of my hands. By seeing the tissue first hand, it allows me to imagine and visualize the tissues as I palpate change in my hands. The visualized images allow me to add intention in a highly specific way that fine-tunes my direction of energy skills and intent.

We do the dissection in layers. First, we palpate the body without cutting anything. On some occasions we have a fixed cadaver (one that has been preserved) as well as one that's unpreserved. This palpation exercise of just feeling fascial glide from the heels of each cadaver offers an amazing dichotomy of textures. One can fully understand how medical providers believe movement of fascia, membranes, and sutures are impossible. If all they have are persevered cadavers and fixed tissue to base their opinions on, I fully understand.

When you as a student hold the unpreserved falx cerebri in your hands, still in place within the skull, and another student puts a torquing manual force in the sacrum, things happen. You feel that, and you start to wonder. When you can see and visualize the change in the falx with your own hands, one can begin to comprehend what is possible with light touch.

Well, that's an interesting exercise, Don, and even a fascinating experience, but will it effect my practice in some way? I am glad you asked. Let me see if I can describe how the palpation experiences in dissection have application in the clinical setting.

I think one of most common clinical complaints I'm asked to address is pelvic pain. It occurs most commonly in women and comes in the form of various diagnoses including dysmenorrhea, ovarian cysts, chronic back pain, endometriosis, status post hysterectomy, or C-section. As I place my hands on the listening stations and then the treatment positions like heels for a still point or pelvic diaphragm for a diaphragm release, I envision the structures I'm about to address. In other words, from the heels, as I begin to feel the fascial planes and arc, I visualize the Achilles tendon gastronemius, hamstrings, sciatic nerve, and the distribution of the corda equina at the distal end of the dural tube. I envision the gentle current of CSF (as I remember we could see it in lab after we exposed the entire dural tube). As I introduce a stillpoint and envision the tube, sometimes I can envision a tension pattern from the heels to T12, (for example) and there it stops. It is at about this time the patient suddenly opens their eyes and says something like, "What's happening, I can feel heat and pulsing in my lower back.

With my hands anterior/posterior on the sacrum and pubis I can envision the uterus. In books it looks like a pear-shaped structure with fallopian tubes and ovaries dangling somewhere in space beside it. In fact the beautiful uterus sits in a large flexible membranous ligamental structure (Broad Ligament) that surrounds the entire inside of the pelvic bowl like a cellophane covering on a kitchen bowl. The ovaries and fallopian tubes are suspended within this broad ligament. I have this picture in my mind, as I follow the first motion of least resistance to end range and plant my gentle barrier. I can sometimes feel the asymmetry of this ligament and can feel a tension pattern, swollen ovary, or adhesional scar tissue. As tissues release, I can feel the structures take a more relaxed seat or position within the pelvis. The patient usually punctuates the release with, "oh" or "wow" or "did you feel that?"

I had a patient some time ago that had lifelong uncontrollable temporal lobe seizures. He had a partial temporal lobectomy.

During the ten-step protocol, after the boney techniques of wobble and finger in the ear, I gently settled into a light touch ear pull. As I engaged the penna cartilage of the ear, I envisioned the temporal bone and its attachment of the tentorium cerebelli at its internal petrous ridge. As I recalled gently pulling on the same spot within the calvarian cut skull in dissection class, I recalled the quality of flexibility in the tentorium. As I held that image in my mind, I held a living tentorium in my hands, by way of the ears. In the subsequent moments, the lighter and longer I held the ears, the more relaxed the tension became, and I could perceive expansion. After the session, the patient reported less head pain and a relief of tingling in his feet. He had better balance, was more relaxed, and has been very pleased with treatment results to date.

In dissection class, we have a full body, and then two separate skulls, one cut in half saggitally and another in the calvarian manner like the skull in the slide presentation of CSTI. If I hadn't seen that, I would not have been able to visualize the changes and, therefore, may have been unwilling to maintain my gentle traction as long as I did.

I frequently have the opportunity to see patients who have had spinal trauma. I think the most common place for dural tube trauma is at the cranial base, where the magnificent skull and brain is membraneously attached to the rest of the spine internally, by the dural tube. Sports injuries, motor vehicle accidents, whiplash, and traumatic birthing can often impart tremendous strain to this area of the spine. Sometimes the menninges is stretched so forcefully in the longitudinal plane that a portion of the brain stem (medulla oblongata) can actually be dislocated and pinned into the foramen magnum. This is often diagnosed as Arnold Chiari Syndrome. Patients range in age from months to decades. It is in dissection that we have the opportunity in the saggital skull and the cadaver body, with the dural tube exposed, to traction the brainstem tissue and cerebellum. I envision this experience as I do my thoracic inlet, hyoid, and OCB release in the clinic on the live patient. I know the dura is just that, durable and strong. And I recall seeing the viability and availability of movement when I manually applied gentle forces from the superior margin inside the skull and then from the tube inferiorly. I remember the ligamental and muscular attachments that made the tube glide slightly within the canal when I pulled on the nuchal ligament and rectus capitus posterior minor muscle in lab. I remember how much force I used to get physiologic change in that tissue. When I am holding a patient on the table, I transfer that lab experience to my fingers. This single intention brings my occipital cranial base release new elements and new results as never before.

One of the major elements of the palpation experience of the dissection class is to remove self-doubt. You all know what I am talking about. Can I really feel the bones move the fascia? Is 5 grams really enough to influence the system? If I mobilize zygoma, will that allow more freedom of movement in the palatines? Can I really traction the dural tube from occiput and feel a restriction somewhere down the tube? How many grams of force on the frontal bone does it take for me to feel anything happen to the falx cerebri?

We do these experiments in class. I have measured grams required with a precise industrial scale. Ranges are from 3 to 35 grams. I know 5 grams is a very valid force because I have seen it change unpreserved lab tissue. Coming away with some of these questions answered in one's own mind not only removes doubt, but also instills confidence and conviction of one's own palpatory abilities, and the principles of Upledger's work.

One of the most far out benefits of the dissection class experience has to do with direction of energy. You will hear Upledger say it for CST, and Barral say it for Viseral Manipulation; you need to know your anatomy. Your hand placement needs to be anatomically correct. Knowledge of anatomy can help you focus the wisdom of the Inner Physician with good intention, streamlined to the appropriate places. This can be amazingly effective as you are calling in stem cells, or as you are working to encourage benign and malignant tissue to diminish, or organ tissue to change from its post-op hypertension.

I had a 30-something-year-old patient that had headaches and ear pain for several months. She had an MRI and was told she had a brain tumor on the inside of her temporal bone. She was placed on medication and sent to me for pain relief. We began with a full 10-step and I showed her the anatomy poster of the cranial membranes and the inside of my plastic skull. I talked to her about direction of energy and said maybe if we both concentrate we could encourage change. We did this for two sessions, one week apart.

She came in for the third session saying she had just returned from Massachusetts Eye and Ear Institute in Boston. She had another MRI and they were to have discussed chemotherapy, radiation, and surgical options. She said it was a very long appointment. They had 6 physicians look at the new MRI and compared it to the first one. They all agreed that what they had first thought was a tumor was now collagen tissue unraveling along the petrous portion of the temporal bone. They said she no longer had a brain tumor. It is now just collagen tissue.

So it was the anatomical orientation from Dissection class that we both could concentrate on and focus our intention. I recall many times seeing heavy collagen tissue peeling away from the cerebellar vault surface as the dura forms the lateral sinus of the tentorium cerebelli. It was this dissection experience that helped me describe tissue orientation to the patient so we could accurately focus our intention during visualization and direction of energy. This refines direction of energy to diamond precision.

The Dissection Class is expensive and lasts three days. The time flies by in what seems like moments. But all the awareness and natural blending that results for the students in the appreciation of this human experience remain for the rest of one's life. I don't know how to put a price on that. I am grateful to my teachers, the cadavers, and the Upledger Institute for making possible the opportunity for unpreserved human cadaver dissection. And that's why I teach the class.

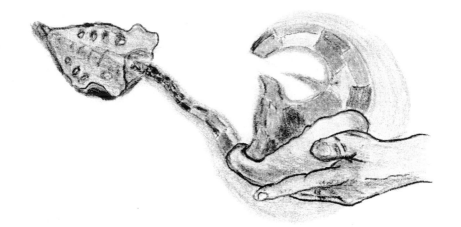

# 5

# Snake Skin Timing

One of the most wonderful aspects of CST is that it has many universal themes that run through the work. One of the truly important procedural elements is timing. Timing is important when a person first decides to have treatment. Planning a schedule for treatment that best suits the patient and the therapist is a time thing. Saying the right words at the right moment is certainly all about timing. And blending touch with intention and holding for moments or minutes is most essential timing.

In class I'm known to repeatedly say, "Time is your ally." I try to drive home the point that practitioners need to allow time for the body to react to the influences of treatment. It takes time for the gentle effects of treatment to facilitate release. Tissue response will be enhanced when one allows time to change tone, lengthen, soften and realign. Cell by cell, fiber by fiber, muscle group, organ fascial plane, one after the other, each react in a cascading effect in response to tissue release over time. If our intention is ultra light touch and to allow time for tissue to respond, wonderful things happen to the body.

Beautiful and amazing things can happen in our physical world as well. We can move through life with less force and we can use the natural tone and structure of things. I inherited a metal trivet from my grandmother's kitchen that says, "Ve get to soon olt, unt too late smart!" It hangs on my wall chiding all who see the words that as we get older we need to make use of every biochemical advantage.

I had a wonderful person who worked with me for twenty years as my assistant, she organized files, arranged patient schedules, and also did a number of mundane things like washing treatment linen and emptying the kitchen garbage. I remember she complained to me that her back was sore after she strained to remove the plastic bag from the plastic rectangular kitchen garbage can. It was mainly paper and therefore packed tightly, so there was little space between the bag and the inside of the can. She strained and pulled hard to get it to come out. I tried it and found it was difficult and a strain......unless......I took my time; and slow......ly pulled......gent......ly. The bag would slowly, gently, move up and out of the can, with a lot less effort then before.

I am always so happy and feel so rewarded, as a teacher, when I receive a letter from a student about how he/she was able to apply what they had learned in class to their real world, especially about timing.

Recently, I received a letter from Jody from Vermont. She said she greatly enjoyed CSTI. A couple of days after the class, she was doing some gardening for her neighbor who had a garden along a stonewall that was known to be home for snakes. She came across a snakeskin that had been shed sometime in the summer. She said she is a bit squeamish with any live snake underfoot, but this skin, she just had to pick up and investigate.

A snake sheds its skin by going through a narrow space between the base of a plant and/or a rock. It sheds its skin at least once a year as a form of renewal for damaged scales. A discarded skin is a nearly clear white semi transparent long tube, conforming to the full length of the snake. This hollow tube is usually compressed in an accordion fashion, and left compressed in the tight place where it was shed.

Jody, in her attempt to view the skin in its extended length nearly ripped through it, even though she was careful. Then she remembered from class the ultra gentle touch and to go slow and allow time to be your ally. She remembered that if she set her intention to go slow and gentle the tissue would change. Very gently gram by gram and extremely slowly, she managed to stretch the snakeskin to its full length. "It literally opened up one scale at a time; it was a fascinating experience—nothing in the world could have taught me more precisely that lesson in ultra gentle touch and intention."

The lesson from the session here is: Just like Jody experienced, CST affords us continuous reminders about our physical world, and can often help us in our activities of daily living. The right amount of force at the right location over an ample period of time can quite literally make you more comfortable in the skin you are in, and it can take the garbage out.

# Part II

## Our Current Medical Model

# 6

# I'll Take Arthritis

*I* was paging through the March 24, 2003 issue of *Time* magazine the other day and I turned to a three-page ad on pages 66, 67, and 68 with the beautiful Olympic skating champion Dorothy Hamill gliding along on the ice with her arms like wings and a big smile. The ad said, "Morning pain can't keep me from doing what I love. Vioxx provides powerful 24-hour relief of Osteoarthritis." It went on to say Vioxx is a prescription medication for arthritis pain and stiffness.

Then I turned the page. It was all text. I measured the print and it was 1/16th of an inch. Vioxx on the opposite page was 1/2 inch print. The third text page gave a list of possible side effects of Vioxx.

They included, serious stomach problems, intestinal bleeding, that In severe cases can lead to hospitalization or death, heart attack, serious allergic reaction which may cause difficulty breathing or swallowing, severe skin reactions have also been reported. Serious kidney problems, including acute kidney failure, or worsening of chronic kidney failure. Sever liver problems, including hepatitis, jaundice and liver failure. Other side effects that have been reported include anxiety, blurred vision, colitis, confusion, depression, fluid change in the lungs, hair loss, hallucinations, low blood cell counts, menstrual disorder, palpitations, pacreatitis. Increased blood pressure, unusual headache with stiff neck, (aseptic meningitis), and vertigo.

More common but less serious side effects with Vioxx have included upper and/or lower respiratory infection, headache, swelling of the legs or feet, back pain, tiredness and urinary tract infections.

Are You Kidding Me!!??......???

Have we come to a time when an allopathic medical treatment is as big or bigger risk to our health than the problem it is supposed to address??????

The article went on to ask what else can one do to manage arthritic pain, and offered exercise, controlling weight, hot and cold treatments, and the use of support devices.

Incidentally, I want to add that CranioSacral Therapy is a gentle manual technique that is helpful with pain and stiffness caused by arthritis. Side effects commonly include a deep state of relaxation, decreased pain, increased range of motion, improved circulation, a feeling of increased energy and well-being. The greatest risk to undergoing CranioSacral Therapy is sleep. It is non-addictive, biodegradable, and non-polluting. It does not have to be taken with water or meals; however there is no reason those activities should be avoided. In the event you have any of these side effects after a CranioSacral Therapy treatment, contact your doctor.

# 7

# The Great American Insurance Paradox

Nowhere else on earth is there a society so influenced by insurance as the United States of America. I believe the paradox is that insurance makes people sick and prevents people from getting well. Let me try to explain.

What is insurance? Well, the dictionary defines it as "a contract binding a company to indemnify an insured party against specific loss," "a protective measure or device." Indemnity is compensation for damage, loss, or injury suffered." A paradox is "a statement that appears to contradict itself or the contrary to common sense but that may be true."[1]

In order to compensate someone for damage loss or injury, one of those negative occurrences needs to happen. Considering the enormous size of the insurance industry in America, the implied risk to life for each and every citizen seems huge. I mean look at the protection from harm one needs just to live and work, own a home, and start a family. One needs life insurance, health insurance, and homeowners insurance for fires, theft, and earthquakes. Then there's flood insurance, auto insurance (with casualty, no fault, and other liability options). There's medical insurance, workers comp insurance, dental insurance, Medicare and supplemental insurance to cover anything Medicare may not. There is travelers insurance, credit card insurance and now most

---

[1] *American Heritage Dictionary*

53

chain stores carry optional extended warrantee coverage, which is a form of insurance. And since 9/11, business property owners are being offered terrorist coverage. Health care providers also have malpractice insurance, that's a big one! Other western nations don't have so much insurance. Why do we?

If I had just landed in this country with my family and was informed about all the insurance I had to purchase just to live here, I'd turn around. If I didn't leave I'd buy a gun and put it by my bed for added insurance protection, in case my home security system failed. Maybe that's why so many homeowners are shot with their own weapon?

All this effort, investment, and constant solicitation implies great risk. If our intention is focused on fear about all the risk there is in our daily lives, our level of anxiety, stress, and tension rises. Our Reticular Alarm System (RAS), that is, our state of vigilance in order to fight or flight in the name of danger, goes way up. We are not at ease in our bodies. Not being at ease, our bodies begin to enter states of disease. Are insurance worries giving us disease? Are insurance companies making people ill by scaring them about their health?

It is wonderful we have health insurance to protect us when we get sick or injured. Truly we need broken bones mended and tissue repaired when traumatic injury occurs. Insurance pays for allopathic medicine, that is, medication to dull our sensation of pain and discomfort. Or in the worst cases, surgery to fix, remove, or replace the organ that is so disturbed it no longer functions. Insurance has a place in our lives, but maybe not as large a place as it does now.

Health insurance has defined how much it costs to cover this benefit. Health insurance is a very unique form of business. The consumer pays them; the insurance company pays the healthcare provider for treatment delivered. This arrangement is like paying a company money, (a lot of money) to hire a plumber to fix your kitchen faucet if it starts to leak. This company tells the plumber what to do. They tell the plumber to replace the faucet washer. The plumber says the entire faucet needs to be replaced to get at the source of the problem. But the insurance company says we will only pay to replace the washer. If the plumber goes ahead and replaces the whole faucet, insurance will not pay him. And since he is a preferred plumbing provider with their network, he is not allowed to charge the homeowner extra for a new faucet.

The plumber says, "but the leak is at the base of the faucet and water has been dripping on the floor now for three years since I replaced the washer. The long term slow leak caused the tile floor in the kitchen to heave up and come apart."

The insurance company now says plumbing insurance does not cover tile. They will not pay for the damage to the floor caused by the leaking faucet. The homeowner will now have to call the store where the faulty tile was purchased. The storeowner, who receives the call, calls his business liability insurance company. They hear the complaint and say nothing is wrong with the product. The tile was improperly laid without underwater glue and the homeowner should contact either their homeowners insurance or the tile installer's malpractice insurance. Are you becoming stressed listening to this? Does this sound familiar? This is why I believe health insurance makes people sick and keeps people from getting well.

You would think health insurance would be a vehicle for people to receive prompt medical care. Well, insurance companies have contractual agreements with providers that stipulate how much the provider is paid, and how much the provider can charge. They dictate the course of treatment in terms of frequency of visits per week and/or total number of visits per diagnosis. They tell the provider what diagnoses that provider is allowed to treat. And, frequently, with primary care physicians, they have capitation clauses in their contracts. They say, "Dr. Xyz, thank you for becoming one of our preferred providers. For that privilege we are providing you with $500,000.00 of physical therapy services you can issue to your patients. We want you to be in charge of your own practice, doctor. We want you to decide who needs care and distribute the P.T. benefit to your patients as you see fit. And the special feature of this contract, doctor, is that any money left at the end of the year, that you don't use for physical therapy for your patients, you get to keep. How does that sound doctor?"

With capitation contracts for services, how much service goes undelivered? Are insurance companies prohibiting patients they insure from receiving care? Are doctors tempted to not provide service for the incentive of financial gain? If capitation contracts cover all the physicians in a geographical area of a specific P.T., is that not an impedance to free trade for the physical therapist? Is that not a Monopolistic Trade Practice? Is that not against the law? Is that not artificially limiting care and preventing patients from getting the treatment they need to get well?

I have worked with patients for a certain length of time. I may have them come in for six visits. I use CranioSacral Therapy and maybe moist heat and massage for 3–4 visits to reduce pain and promote healing. I then begin to help them move and regain function with exercise. They become 75% better, but then they run out of visits covered by insurance. The insurance company says the statistical average number of visits for that particular diagnosis is 6. Therefore, that's all they will pay. As the physical therapist, I have a dilemma. I can discharge them from my service knowing that treatment is incomplete. Or I can continue to treat them another 2–4 visits, complete the service to regain function and teach them home exercises to stay healthy. But, I do not get paid for those last few visits. And my insurance contract prohibits me from asking the patient to pay for them. This scenario occurring frequently in a busy single practice like mine quickly puts me in cash flow jeopardy.

Sometimes treatment goes the other way. Some insurances pay for 30 visits of physical therapy for a single diagnosis in a calendar year. I have had a few patients who are fully healed but want to continue with treatment because it feels good. When the patient pays several hundred dollars per month for medical insurance, they feel justly entitled to treatment when prescribed by their physician. Occasionally as I deliver physical therapy and they feel better, more relaxed, less painful, and happier; they don't want to stop. I've had people say, "I feel so good I want to come as long as my insurance will allow. They rationalize that they have paid $500.00 per month for the last three years, haven't had medical services in that time so they are entitled to: 500 x 12 = 6000.00 x 3 years = 18000.00 of my services. I am then in a position of saying your goals are met, you are painfree and have full range of motion so we must stop; or continue. Are insurance companies preventing people from getting well by not covering enough therapy? Are they providing so much coverage, that patients intentionally don't get well in order to receive the maximal number of sessions?

I think insurance companies set their criteria for service based on their own fear factor. They fear health practitioners will bilk the system and treat people longer than they have to. If only they could let go of that fear and realize most of us don't do that— most of us don't have time for that. Insurance companies have created such fear in our culture that we have more stressed out people than we can possibly handle. There is no incentive to treat each patient longer than absolutely necessary.

I know several emergency room physicians. They are fearful of lawsuits and the rapid increase in medical malpractice lawsuits. Again, the insurance industry is influencing another part of the population with fear. In an effort to avoid a lawsuit and have on record proof that every possible diagnostic test was done, many physicians are ordering CT scans, MRIs, x-rays, lab work, and diagnostic ultrasound. These tests are sometimes being ordered not out of medical necessity but to ensure the physician doesn't get sued. Typically, a radiologist with a specialty in MRI interpretation is employed to read films that are not medically necessary. The workload goes up as well as fatigue and chance of error. Accuracy goes down. So extra tests and procedures are being done to ensure the physician doesn't go to court. Here's another way in which the insurance industry has indirectly caused a failure in the medical system to treat the people who really need treatment. If a doctor does get sued, their malpractice insurance increases since the insurance company now views that doctor as an increased risk and liability to indemnify. Extra procedures produce extra costs, and as they say in the insurance business, "increased financial exposure." These increased costs are passed on to the patient, the employer, the business owner, and the employee who makes payments. The cycle of fear spirals higher and more out of control.

To cover the added expense, workload, and patient population, hospitals are building additions, hiring more staff, and buying more equipment. Work overload and delivery costs go up. Costs are passed on to the consumer. The consumer employs the insurance company to pay for these increases. Insurance companies pass the increase on to consumers in 20–30% increases in policy costs each year. Can anyone see the cycle of destructive, chaotic behavior here based on fear, greed, and power? Are insurance companies making people sick and keeping people from getting well? Yes they are!

What is the cure for this disease? I believe the cure is to radically reform the system. Allow care providers to provide the care they think people need. Pay providers an hourly salary based on expertise, experience, and skill level. Pay all providers equally. That is, pay private practice therapists the same as hospital based therapists. Remove all capitation and allow physicians to refer patients to therapies and treatment they honestly feel they need medically without financial incentive either way. Prohibit physician owned physical therapy and other therapy services to avoid financial incentive for referrals. Encourage wellness and wholeness as a part of standard healthcare. Encourage natural whole foods with the least amount of preservatives. Promote movement and exercise as a requirement for insurance coverage for all covered persons. Incorporate stress reduction into all forms of employment and work. Provide stress reduction techniques like drinking water, walking, meditation, breath venting, and quiet reflection as part of work and home environments. Empower people to care for themselves with home exercises, lifting and body mechanics, and balanced diet instruction. Set up hot lines in insurance companies to counsel on wellness, stress reduction, and nutrition. Insurance companies and hospitals now have hot lines to discuss coverage and bill paying questions. How about a health hot line as a standard service 24/7?

Promote a healing environment with soft lighting, soothing music, and colorful surroundings. Encourage human contact like massage, CST, therapeutic touch, walking, and exercise assistance. As patients leave hospitals, prescribe home exercise and living adaptations that avoid injury, promote movement, relaxation and good nutrition. Most patients now leave the hospital with only prescriptions for medications that insurance only partially pays for.

Teach the patients to care for themselves. "An ounce of prevention is worth a pound of cure." Teach patients they are real people, responsible for their bodies. They must use good judgement and will, to decide what they eat and drink and how they move their physical body units. Willpower, intention, and intuition are conscious activities that need to be employed and cultivated in order to prevent harm from happening around us. That's our indemnity. This is our protective device. That's real natural insurance.

The lesson I've learned personally and from my many sessions with my patients is: We are all dying. Each day brings us closer to that mystical moment when we drop our body and move on. No insurance policy can prevent that. No policy should. When there is no more life to live, death is a wonderful alternative. Would you rather sit in a nursing home in a worn out body indefinitely? We all need to let go of our fear of death and this American Insurance fear of life and try to live this time allowed to each of us as best we can. Pursue happiness in the most peaceful and harmless way possible. Respect, honor, and treat others as you would want to be treated. Move through your life with love and not fear. Insure yourself. Live consciously and do the right thing.

# 8

# Beyond Diagnosis

*T*he Greek definition of diagnosis is: to distinguish. *Taber's Medical Dictionary* describes it as the recognition of a disease from its symptoms, a formal statement of the decision reached in identifying a disease. Greek physicians had obviously been doing that. Physicians commonly identified physical symptoms and complaints and associated them with a certain cause. Common remedies were then prescribed. The Greek physician Hippocrates (the Father of Medicine) is credited with prescribing preventative medicine of exercise, diet, and massage in the sixth century B.C.

In the 19th century A.D. and beyond, things changed. Physicians were charged with making "differential diagnosis" and prescribing the "cure." Allopathic medicine was born and has been the modern standard of medicine in the western world for the last 100 years or so. Allopathy is defined as the science of treating a disease by inducing effects different from those produced by the disease. That means if something makes you bleed, you try to stop the bleeding. If you are too hot, we try to cool you down. If you have pain we try to stop it. The methodology became characteristic by the 1950s in two major ways. If you had a symptom, you were given a medication to take it away. If the medication didn't stop the problem, it would be surgically cut out.

This system seemed to have relative success until two things happened (in my opinion). First came the 1960s. PEACE NOW,

FREE LOVE, NO MORE WAR. Suddenly people began returning to natural thinking and questioning our culture. We began to self assess and question our cultural norms of allopathy versus mind/body connection, true happiness, wellness, and the meaning of life. These new thoughts were punctuated by Pop Music, which introduced us to meditation, mind/body exercise, like yoga, and Tai Chi. Medicine was also introduced in a popular way to vegetarianism, massage, gestalt psychotherapy, aerobics, jogging, and transcendental meditation; and there was new and popular interest in osteopathy, chiropractic, and physical therapies. And of course we know many of the elements of CranioSacral Therapy were established in the early 70s. Since that time people have begun to better understand their bodies. Old ideas are resurfacing like those of Hippocrates about diet and exercise;.A. T. Still's notion that the body is a unit, functioning as a whole; and we have Upledger saying that we should listen to our bodies, as our bodies really know how to heal themselves.

Even in the *Journal of the American Medical Association* (Nov. 1998) change was acknowledged. (Visits to practitioners of alternative therapy in 1997 exceeded the projected number of visits to all primary care physicians in the United States by an estimated 243 million.) (In 1990 an estimated one in five individuals seeing a medical doctor for a principal condition also used an alternative therapy. This percentage increased to nearly one in three by 1997.)

The other major event that occurred in the world was digitalization and the computer. Information that had been doubling in the world every 30 years by the 1940s was now doubling every seven to nine months. The result from the 1970s until now (2004) is that we have more choices. Many of the jobs, services, and products we now depend on weren't even invented in 1950. Witness the computer, the laptop, Palm Pilots, cell phones, T.V. remote controls, Nintendo, microwave ovens, electric windows, toothbrushes, shavers, hair dryers, cassette tapes, CDs and DVDs, and answering machines. Occupations have experienced profound change and new inventions including: personal trainer, interior designer, dietitian, computer programmer, telemarketer, financial advisor, human resource consultant, marketing consultant, advertising agent, multi-media programmer, CEO, CFO, legal advisor, patient advocate, domestic engineer, marriage counselor, sex therapist and clinical coordinator. Even services and businesses have changed. Most of the products and services we use now weren't available back in the fifties. Wal-Mart, Staples, Nissan, Mitsubishi, Honda, Suzuki, Fiji film, Microsoft, AOL.com, Nike, US Air, Verizon and MCI are just a few examples.

The point here is we have so many choices, distractions and sheer volume of activities to consume our lives that most of us suffer from stress. Many medical authorities site stress as an underlying cause for most medical visits. When that happens we become less at ease in our bodies and therefore more at risk for disease. Chronic headaches, fibromyalgia, arthritis, forward head posture, carpal tunnel syndrome, chronic back pain, TMJ dysfunction, and anxiety are all diagnoses influenced by stress. One of the major reasons people don't respond to allopathic medicine if they have one of these diagnoses is because taking a pill or having a portion of your body cut off or taken out won't remove the stress produced in your body by our modern lives. Our diagnoses are really symptoms of our culture and have to do with anxiety, sadness, fear, loss of hope, anger, lack of well-being, heartache, jealousy, and malnourishment.

The other very interesting thing about diagnosis is the intention of it. That is, the purpose and what it means to you to be diagnosed. Deepak Chopra has an interesting story about that. He tells of an indigenous culture in New Zealand in which the Shaman or medicine man is the most powerful person in the village. If a person is severely harmed by another, maliciously, such as a family member killed or wife raped, the complaint is brought to the shaman. He will consult his spiritual powers and if he finds that the complaint is valid and of truth, he provides a remedy. He gives his sacred blessing and power in a ceremony and then gives a blessed hollow bone to the person with the complaint. That person is to go to the person who did him grievous deadly harm and he is to shake the bone at the perpetrator.

It is well known throughout that culture that anyone who has a hollow bone (blessed and empowered by a Sharman) shaken at them will die in 48 hours. In this culture spontaneous death occurs within 48 hours 100% of the time.

How is this possible? I believe the trigger for the event is intention. I think the conscious notion that a person of great power, knowledge, wisdom, and authority has decreed you are to die (in this New Zealand culture), then that is enough of an intention to cause the body to bring the event to reality. If this is so, what happens in our culture if a person of authority tells us that we have a terminal condition?

The big question is, does a medical diagnosis actually, intentionally, stimulate the symptoms of disease? Terminal cancer must mean I have to die from this! Does diagnosis stimulate the progress? It doesn't have to be death. Authoritative words like Degenerative Arthritis, Degenerative Disc Disease, Chronic Fatigue Syndrome, Chronic Heart Failure, Pulmonary Insufficiency, Respiratory Failure, Developmental Defects, Ovarian Dysfunction, Mental Deficiency, Mental Retardation—do these not predicate an outcome? By providing a diagnosis from a person of authority in our culture, are we not setting the intention for terminality, degeneration, dysfunction, insufficiency or failure?

I really abide by the practice of Dr. Upledger in requesting the diagnosis be withheld, at least until he has had a chance to put his hands on the patient and listen to the body. How many of us would have missed the origin of a problem if we had just delivered treatment to the diagnosed area?

Sometimes the patient is saying, "Well, the doctor said I will never be able to do this and that," or "there is no cure" or "I will just have to live with it." I tell the patient "Hey, I believe you know your body better than anybody. How about if we give your body a chance to heal? Could you leave the window of that opportunity open for your body? Could we just listen to your body and go where it tells us and see what happens? If you can't do this or that you'll know it before anyone has to tell you. Let's see what happens, okay?"

Lesson from many sessions here is: We can't do much about a diagnosis the patient comes in with except not trust it. Move beyond the diagnosis with good intention and give the body a chance to speak.

# 9

# Don't Know Mind

/t seems to me that this topic of CranioSacral Therapy is very strange. I mean here we are doing something with the body using 5 grams (the weight of a nickel) of manual pressure. We are listening to the body. We are feeling for the rhythm of fluid coursing through the body. We are talking to body parts and actually encouraging the body to change.

Oftentimes people come to us after exhausting all other avenues of treatment in the conventional sense. They may have had a poor surgical outcome or developed intolerance to medication or other procedure. Frequently they have spent a lot of time and their own money trying to find a "cure" for their problems, having gone to specialists in major cities and of different disciplines. Their primary care physician may send them to an orthopedist, who sends them to a neurologist, who sends them to an internist, who sends them to an allergist. In each case they seek a medical opinion, a diagnosis and curative treatment. They want someone to "Just Fix It."

What a strange thing it is then, when an individual asks the medical person if they can help and the answer is "I don't know." They may continue with questions such as "Well what is my diagnosis?"

"I don't know."

"When will I know if this is going to help me?"

"I don't know."

"Will I ever get better?"

"I don't know."

What do you know? It is here in this neutral place that there is only one position to take as a CST practitioner.

"I don't know what is wrong with you."

"I don't know if I can help."

"I do know I cannot heal or cure you."

"I do know I can listen to your body and encourage release, relaxation, and constructive change."

Being in the space of Don't Know Mind, I believe is very unique and beneficial for the patient. It is particularly antithetical after suffering a physical problem and then investing months or years in time and energy seeking a medical opinion.

If a person has a headache, neck, or right shoulder pain, the usual medical evaluations, tests and diagnostic procedures are focused on the site of the problem. Patients quickly get categorized, referred, and referenced as that headache patient, neck injury person, or shoulder problem. When patients come to us, apparently that approach hasn't worked. We can use the same approach—or would it be better to try a new and different way of looking at the body?

John Upledger's description of how he approaches his patients is interesting. People from all over the world come to him at his Health Plex Clinic in Palm Beach Gardens, Florida. Often they bring with them a portfolio of x-rays, MRIs, CT scans, lab work and numerous consultants' reports. When they come to see John, he is courteous and kind and listens to their introduction. But then he often interrupts them. He says something like this.

"I see you've been to many places and have been seen by many specialists and they all have their findings. I am sure they are in great detail and I will review them later if you wish. However, you have come here to see if I might be able to help you. In order for me to do that, I would like to look at you in a different way. I want to evaluate you as a whole person and evaluate your body by listening to the way your entire system works. I need to be open to the possibility that your problem may have an origin that is somewhere else in your body other than where your pain is. I don't want to know what others have found before I have a chance to make some observations of my own. Is it okay if you just lie down here and let me see what I can see?"

I have seen him do this several times and I am amazed for several reasons. First, because he can begin at a place of not knowing. It takes bravery to step into the future on an adventure into the unknown, when you are consulted and retained to define the unknown. Once a practitioner can get past the fear of that, there is great freedom in it. To be in Don't Know Mind means that you are free to come to your own conclusions. The honesty of this approach is really attractive to me. Here one person (the patient) is willing to lie down and be assessed. Here another person (the therapist) places hands on, with no preconditions, judgments, and simply attempts to get quiet and listen to what the body is trying to reflect. This is in the tradition of A.T. Still in the 1880s when he said the body is a unit and structure follows function. A person may carry their head and neck to one side because they have a stone in their shoe. Unless you look at the whole person you will miss that alignment orientation of their posture as they limp with partial weight bearing on one leg. Working on the neck may provide temporary relief but it will not address the origin of the problem. Someone needs to remove the stone in the shoe at the other end of the body. This whole body approach applies to many orthopedic problems.

Take for example heel spurs in the foot and calcium build up on the acromion of the shoulder. In the heel spurs, weight bearing and ambulation is commonly with a heavy heel strike. This strains the plantar intrinsic muscles of the sole of the foot at their attachment at the calcaneous. The body tries to lay down more bone to keep the muscle attachment from pulling out. The calcium forms a pinnacle out of the tendon (spur) and one steps on that with each foot strike causing painful results. Making changes in gait and losing weight can cause the body to stop laying down bone because pressure on the calcaneal tendon insertion diminishes.

In the instance of shoulder pain and x-ray confirmation of calcium build up, a similar event is occurring. The glenoid fossa or shoulder socket is rather flat to accommodate the large round head of the humerus as it rolls around. Close to the glenoid fossa (shoulder socket) is where several muscles attach to the scapula (shoulder blade). The scapula has bony prominences for the muscle attachments. The major ones are the acronion and the glenoid process. If someone has forward head posture and forward rounded shoulders as their normal posture, shoulder alignment is altered. As the large upper arm bone (humerus) moves when the arm goes over the head, it strikes the out of position acromion. Over time stress occurs to the bone and the body lays down more bone to protect itself. Calcium develops on the acromion. This is not a flaw of the body, but the body's attempt to protect itself. That's why with heel spur surgery and acromoplasty surgery calcium grows back in 50% of the cases. If we encourage postural changes and improve joint alignment the problems subside.

I have many times evaluated the patient as a whole person and the patient has asked, often to their surprise, "Excuse me Mr. Ash, but my doctor sent me here for you to help me with my headaches, why are you holding my rear end?"

They seem to suddenly understand when I explain to them, their beautiful nervous system circulates its fluid (CSF) for nutrition and well-being by gently moving the inner membranes attached to the bones of the head and the tail (sacrum). If for some reason the tailbone gets jammed and it can't move, the bones and membrane attachments at the other end of the system can strain trying to accommodate the motion required to circulate this central nervous system nutritional fluid. By insuring both ends of the system have freedom of movement, balance is attained, and pain, stiffness, and dysfunction abate.

Commonly, the patient may suddenly say, "I fell on my rear end on the ice getting out of my car. You know, that's when my headaches started. I had forgotten about that."

So how long does the therapist stay in Don't Know mind? Until about now. Once the patient comes to the awareness of the origin of the injury, the therapist now can just concentrate on encouraging change and release. We monitor for change and reevaluate the rhythm. We may also talk to them about posture and exercise. When the rhythm has returned in the sacrum and the patient is pain free, we wish them a happy life.

"Don, do you think this will ever happen to me again?"

"I don't know!"

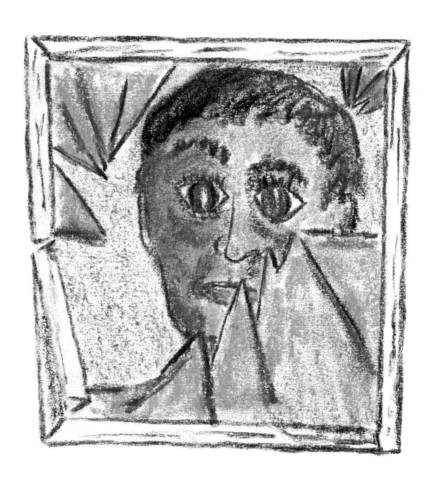

# 10

# Broken Glass

*H*ey! Accidents happen. Bad things happen to good people and timing is always the worst. When this happens, lives become broken. Activities change or cease. The structure of our lives breaks and is in pieces. Relationships change between the victim, their bodies, their families, their employers, themselves. Sometimes those features of a life, thought to be solid, stable, and structured, simply shatter and fall apart.

Trauma fractures bones as well as thought processes, leaving cracks in the matrix of both calcium and cerebrum. Equilibrium, vision, personality, logic, receptive and expressive wording, emotions; all these can be chipped and damaged. Memory can be distorted and severely altered both in the brain and the body. The shear recall of the trauma can cause such fear as to render the body tense, painful, spasmodic, and dysfunctional. The memory of the event can be so horrific as to make a person cry, cringe, and turn away from the image and try to push away or bury any recall. If trauma comes from a common thing like broken glass, the memory of it may cause a person to be frightened to ride in a car or look out a window. Physical and mental memory effects can be incapacitating to normal living.

As all this relates to CranioSacral Therapy, we use our hands very gently and lightly to listen to the body. We evaluate how trauma is reflected in the gentle rhythmic movement of the central nervous system. And then we use our hands at strategic positions on the body to encourage change, releasing the effects of trauma; be they energetic, visceral, musculoskeletal, mental, or emotional.

CranioSacral Therapy has standards and common characteristics that we objectify like symmetry quality, amplitude, and rate. But the work also is very individualized; body and hand positions are as different as the infinite variety of shapes of broken glass.

Helping people pick up the pieces of their broken lives vary also. The image that came to me one morning was a baseball accidentally thrown through a garage door window. Glass pieces of random shape, size, and number lie all about the cement floor.

Now who picks up the pieces? Do you make the kid do it? Do you do it yourself? Or, do you do it together, double checking for a piece that may have been far flung and could hurt someone at a later date? Do you pick up the big pieces on the floor first, or do you remove the sharp shards still left in the windowpane?

As it relates to CranioSacral Therapy, there are different ways to approach things. The therapist can work on the structural relief, helping the inertia of the traumatic event vacate the body in the form of heat, pulsing, or gentle little muscle fasciculation's (Krya). The tissue release can help the person relax, rest, and heal. And sometimes the therapist needs to encourage the patient to go deep within and recognize why there remains such an ache in the heart or deep internal pain in the pelvis. The body leads the way with still points that draw attention to a body part or position in which memory of trauma resides. If we take our time and allow the memory to come to conscious awareness, the patient is able to release it. Emotions of guilt, shame, sadness, and fear are as important to fix for the baseball thrower as the glass repair for the garage owner. If the ball thrower knows he/she is safe and won't get into trouble, they are free to express themselves, and thereby able to release those negative emotions, if they are there. As we would deal kindly with a young person who may have just broken a window; we can extend the same courtesy to the person on our table. If we remain impartial, non-judgmental, ego subordinate, and unconditionally present, the truth will become clear.

As in the garage, working together, we can gently and carefully pick up the broken glass. If we grab quick or hard, we can cut ourselves. If we go slow and gently, look for pieces on the ground, listen for crunching under our feet, we can find it all. If we use care and gentle urgings, we can encourage those broken shards still in the window frame to come free. This opens space for a new window to replace the broken glass and, once again, the view outside can become clear and we can see tomorrow. The lesson here is sometimes accidents offer a unique opportunity to work one on one with those who have had their lives broken or shattered. Where, why, when, and how the glass got broken makes each CranioSacral Therapy session an adventure.

# 11

# Healing Crisis

One of the best parts of advanced cranial work as taught by the UI is that the training requires *you* to do *your own* work. It is with the help of others who are learning and willing to do their own work, that each of us has an opportunity to look at ourselves from different angles offered by the gentle urgings of the CS rhythm. Having said that, it is our decision and ours alone to look, or not to look, at what our bodies are showing us.

I was reminded by a patient today about healing crisis. It refreshed memories of my own healing crisis and essentially the healing that took place because of it.

In my case, I was working as a physical therapist director of rehab services in a small hospital, a part–time home care therapist, a columnist for a local newspaper, a school board member, a volunteer fireman, sheep farmer, husband and father. To say I was unable to recognize that my life was too hectic was an understatement. So my body tried to help me.

In order for me to see the light, my body gave me a healing crisis. First, I came down with gallbladder disease. So I said, "Okay, take it out and I'll stay home a couple weeks, but then I gotta get back to business." I went back to my schedule and came down with mononucleosis. "Okay," I said, "I'll rest a couple of weeks, but then I gotta get back to work. I've got places to go and people to see."

Then my body became more impatient. I came down with pneumonia and I couldn't breath. My body was telling me I had to change or go home. No amount of medication or medical intervention in the past twelve months could persuade my body to stop getting my attention. By the way, the pneumonia caused me to cancel a scheduled continuing education course on fascial release work. If someone were to look at my life back in 1987, they would have seen a very successful, committed, highly functioning individual who was taking part in his community and prospering. But the fact is, that life was killing me.

So, I finally realized that I had to alter my life. I was doing too much, moving too fast, and not taking time to balance my life with work, rest, and play. My wonderful body wouldn't stop until I learned this lesson. It needed the length of time it took to break me down. My recovery from pneumonia also coincided with the next available class of fascial release work in my area. The year was 1987, and it was sponsored by an institute I hadn't heard of before. It was the Upledger Institute. So began the process of my healing that forced me to rise out of three health crisises to redirect my life. I now know that moving from my very data-based, high stress, institutional setting to having a small CranioSacral practice in an old farm house brought me full circle. Had rapid recovery from my physical problems been achieved with medications, I might not have had the time I needed to process the stress factors in my life, nor discover my passion for the work known as CST.

The lesson from the session here is, it's okay if all of your patients don't have immediate positive response to your treatment. They may be in a healing crisis. Their bodies may need you (the therapist) *to be unsuccessful* in order to allow the patient more time to process the issues of their life. Pain may be a gift from the body encouraging them to change. If we never knew pain, how would we know pleasure? If we never learned bad, how could we recognize good? If we didn't have night, how could we know the absence of darkness is day? How arrogant are we that we think we know what releases need to be released and what emotion needs to be emoted for the greatest good of the patient, and at what time and place this is to occur??

Sometimes the very best we can be; is present. The best we can do; is listen with our hands and facilitate the body to do *what it needs to do* for the patient. It is well to realize that sometimes the best thing we can do for the patient is nothing. Wish them a happy life and move on. In other words, being of no help may be exactly what the patient needs at this time.

As we interact in each other's life, it serves us to realize we can only know that we are somewhere along the patient's path of life. Whether we are on the path or at the crossroads is the great mystery that can only happen when we observe the present moment. Sometimes it is our role to encourage the body to show the person the beginning or the end of their path. It is the young expectant mother's healing crisis that causes her cervix to finally give way and the uterus reach a threshold which begins contractions in an effort to expel the fetus. Sometimes it is the fetus who has a hesitancy to come out of their place of comfort and shelter.

As a P.T. specializing in CST I occasionally am asked to try CST on an infant considered hopeless. These young souls all have great trouble in landing here on Earth. I consider them great teachers, considering the fact that most of them are less than 6 months old and already they have confounded the greatest medical centers in the world by their very survival.

I held one little man expected to die in the first week of life. He was born with severe anoxia (lack of oxygen to the brain) after a 40 hour home delivery. He required oral suction every 20 minutes. I held him at 9 weeks old. He came to a still point, arched his back, and moaned for 20 minutes. His moan was a heartache and sorrow for his circumstances. He moaned like an old woman that had just lost a son in the war. It came from his solar plexus.

His lips puckered, his brow furrowed, his fists clenched, and his little body stiffened. He moaned for his circumstance and then for his right to exist. All of us in the room (mom, other therapist, and myself) felt a chill in our spines as he voiced his healing crisis. He is now 1 ½ years old, moving all fours. His eyes track. He laughs. He coos. And who's to say he shouldn't live and continue to teach us that life is precious.

Sometimes a healing crisis is the entrance to our exit here on Earth. As it relates to transition, a healing crisis sometimes is the most moving event to allow the notion of death to descend on the person. You know when there is no more life left to live, death (or transition to another existence) is a wonderful alternative to lingering, suffering, and progressive loss of function. When a person is worn down by age or infirmity and fatigued by sleeplessness and exhausted by struggling for breath, there is a gentle curtain that descends and the person quietly resigns. Struggle stops, pain and the grimacing face subsides and softens. The mind moves from conflict to acceptance, and vision seems to transcend physical space. Often the person in process sees beyond this physicality and describes the great mystery beyond as bright, warm, and pleasant, with friendly loving faces awaiting.

The healing crisis is the catalyst for awareness shift, in that the stimulation doesn't quit, until the patient does, and then there is calm, peace, and transition.

And from personal, first-hand witness experience, I can tell you, after the last breath, and the heart stops, the last physically perceivable movement in the entire body is the cranial rhythm that trails off to a whisper and is gone.

The Chinese express crisis with two symbols, one for danger and one for opportunity. Another lesson from the session here is: We are charged as CST therapists to stand with the patient in the perceived moment of risk and watch for the opportunity to understand and experience this life. Ours is not to know if they are coming or going, only that it is sacred.

# Part III

## Lessons in Structure

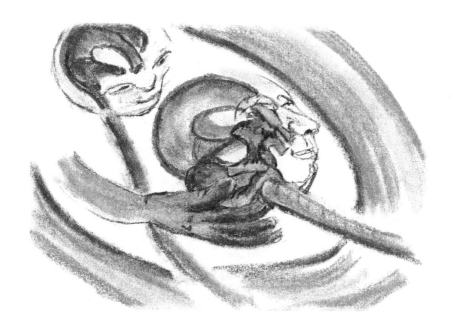

# 12

## Circling

Protocol is a word to bring order to a process. Once one knows the order, with practice, one becomes familiar with the process. It becomes clear that the order of the process is determined by the process. There is a natural order and one made by man. The protocol then is man's attempt to understand the natural process. This applies to weather, water, earth shift, the balance of nature, and all the natural rhythms of the world. No where is it more true than in the intimate rhythms of the human body.

CranioSacral Therapy has within it protocol and order. We have ways of providing options for a process to be understood. It is arrogant and ego generated to think the process can't happen unless the protocol is present. I am reminded each night and day that the moon and the sun were in the process of a circle—and circling long before we thought of the wheel. Man did not invent the wheel, the moon and the sun did.

The more one tries to just observe and learn from the process (such as the CranioSacral Rhythm) the more intimate one becomes with the circular rhythms of life. We then can understand and rest in our natural place within the web.

The protocol we follow as therapists in CST is the 10-Step Protocol—providing an order and means to observe the process of the CranioSacral Rhythm (CSR) as it exists within the physical body. We have the order of listening stations to become the consummate observer. We have the characteristics of rhythm in SQAR (Symmetry, Quality, Amplitude, and Rate) in an attempt to give this natural process order. And we have the 10 steps to provide a method to provide gentle assistance. In it we try to liberate tissue first from the periphery, then the spine, and finally the head, at the sutures and menninges. This is our invention (Dr. John Upledger's).

We are wise to remember as the sun and moon are wheels, the cranial rhythm was a process long before it was invented by man. As planets influence day and night with darkness and light, one can also influence the natural setting of CSR with touch as gentle and as profound. It is most important to understand our process of delivering CST may not be the exact process in the body. As good as we think we are, our protocol is our process for order, not necessarily the body's. Our protocols and methods help give us an understanding of the body's process. Sometimes all of us can become overwhelmed or otherwise separated from our body's natural process. We (patients) need help and solicit the aid of others (therapists) who use a protocol to identify where restrictions are in the body. And sometimes we (therapists) can get so caught up in performing the protocol that we really aren't listening to the body (patient). We (therapists) can even neglect our own body's needs. From time to time therapists need to solicit another therapist so that we can have work done on ourselves and understand our own process.

Beyond the 10-Step Protocol is the protocol of SomatoEmotional Release. As the light of the sun can light up the surface of the earth, we can shine natural energy toward the surfaces of the human body. If we focus our energy of observation (intention) and listen, then with the patient's permission, we can direct energy into the patient. Often there is change in the patient. Hopefully, we have made the patient aware of the process of change in his or her body. And like the circle and the wheel, the patient can rediscover their own body's process.

Our influence, therefore, must be enough to encourage the body's process, but not so much as to throw it off course and prejudice the results with our expectations. Our efforts are gentle urgings in thought, touch, and energy—enough to light the way, but not enough to remove choice and free will of the patient. The sun and the moon shine, but they stay in their place and relinquish final authority to large cycles of season, gravitational forces and the vast circle of our galaxy and universe.

So, the influence of touch can be energetic and our influence of thought can be intention. When we yield to the body's abilities to release, that's indirect technique. When we use gentle influence with grams, it is direct.

Our process widens to yet another dimension of the circle, with dialogue. Words can influence and excite energy in the body, just as brightness of the moon can light a darkened sky and can connote love and romance. It can also foster questioning, fear, and horror for what lies in the darkness beyond the influence of moonlight. Should the patient present in fear and pain, it is our role to aid the process by holding space in thought and positive energy in order for the patient to look into places of fear. If we can act like a flashlight and shine light with neutral words, we can help reveal what is hidden in the deep, dark places. Maybe then fear, shame, guilt, and powerlessness can be put in a different context. Maybe we can help the patient change their process to value fear less and love and understanding more. Surely life is happier when one's glass is half full rather than half empty.

I am reminded to say it is the patient's process and rules of order. Our protocols can only help shine light so they can see. Never should we shine light and tell them what they are looking at or how to value what they are viewing. Nor is it our place as therapists to tell them how long the process should take. I've worked with people who are actively dying and with those left behind grieving. It can take moments, months, or years. It takes as long as it takes. Awareness can come in a moment of rapture and epiphany. Awareness and understanding can also truly require a lifetime of circumstances and gentle urgings. Who are we to judge that process? As therapists we only aid and try to facilitate the process. It is a gentle balance and requires us to be open, clear, responsible, alert, aware, and—most importantly—humbled by the opportunity to witness healing in the present moment.

The final notion about protocol is that it is an invention of man. It is not the process. So, in the final analysis it doesn't exist. And in the end, we use it just to get to the optimal awareness for the patient and therapist. Then we can let it drop away and just witness the truth of real understanding between the patient's heart, mind, and body. We come full circle and sit wondering about the place the strand of our life has in the grand web.

# 13

# Therapeutic Presence, Sexuality, Boundaries

I have heard my mentor and friend Fred Stahlman, P.T., teach CSTI and describe CST as light touch, so light in fact that sometimes there is unearned intimacy.

When people elect to be patients and come for CranioSacral Therapy, oftentimes, they are hurting, with physical and emotional change. They often can be in a healing crisis and their body is simply causing them to stop functioning normally, as they are accustomed. That can mean a dramatic change in status as an employee, spouse, partner, child, or parent. Sometimes people come from a space that has been so painful for so long that the light 5 grams of touch or the gentle prolonged holding of direction of energy or still point, feels really good. It is gentle, soft, safe, comforting, warm, and delivered with good intention. It is such a good feeling that sometimes it feels like a caress. Caress is defined as an act or expression of affection.

Dr. John has often said that as practitioners of CranioSacral Therapy we need to dedicate ourselves to making the world a touch better. It is not a stretch of anyone's imagination to understand that well-intentioned touch is needed to counteract touch that is not well intentioned in this world. One only has to think of words like road rage, prejudice, crack house, domestic violence, shaken baby syndrome, sexual abuse, child abuse, alcoholism, street gangs, Middle East, terrorism, and 9/11, to begin to comprehend the full meaning of Dr. John's words.

I have learned many lessons from my patients over the years, but truly one of the most important for me has been one of holding my own awareness and responsibility in session as it relates to physical contact.

Light touch often equates to caress, physical attraction, and relationships. Holding healthy boundaries in a therapeutic session enables the patient to allow feelings to come forward. If a negative feeling was acquired sexually, then sexuality needs to be explored to facilitate the release. As a practitioner, I continually try to abide by the tenets of CST. [I will be impartial, non-judgmental, ego subordinated and unconditionally present.] If I were not to adhere to those attributes, I would be attracted to the patient and not be impartial. I would judge the patient's attractiveness and would not be non-judgmental. If I were to contemplate whether the patient finds me attractive I would not be subordinating my ego. If I were thinking about all those things in session, I would not be unconditionally present, would I???

Susan Scurlock-Durana, is a senior teacher for the UI and developer of the Healing from the Core workshops. She has identified five basic principles in holding a therapeutic presence for a session, which are wonderful:

◊ Holding therapeutic pressure is a state of being, not doing. In this state of being you feel connected, full of your own energy, and present for the other person.

◊ Recognize your own energy level. Do your own work to energize yourself. Acknowledge your skills and talents, and trust your intuition.

◊ Access your own source of energy and stay grounded and full so as not to take on any of the patient's discharging anxiety, fear, pain, grief, etc.

◊ Remember you are holding a space of unconditional love, acceptance, and a vision of wholeness for that person. Hold that space of unconditional love for yourself as well. You can feel empathy for what the person is going through but remain in your own energy.

◊ Remember your body is a finely tuned instrument and navigational system. Stay in it, even if the patient goes out of theirs.

One of the strongest human emotions is love. One way love is expressed is by touch. Ultimate love touch is the sacred union of sex. When sex is received with negative touch and unwelcome force, as in molestation and/or rape, negative emotions are transmitted to different parts of the body like the pelvis, face, and chest. As our Dr. John defines it, "energy cysts" form and lead to dysfunction, and it is through the gentle compassionate light touch of CST that negative emotions are released.

At those moments of release, the patient may have feelings of relief, peace, joy, gratitude, and affection. Sometimes the heart opens and warm pleasant feelings (sometimes absent for a long time) flood the space.

It is at this time that an association of light touch raises feelings expressed as sexual attraction. It is in these moments that a patient may say to you, the therapist,

"I have strong feelings for you."

"I think I am falling in love with you."

"I am on fire."

"I love you."

As a practitioner, what do you do with this? Over a period of multiple sessions you may have cultivated the same feelings. Once in a career, if both you and the patient are not in a committed relationship, it may be an opportunity to find your life partner. If it happens once a year, you, the therapist, need to work on yourself to understand your feelings, those of others, and setting boundaries. Get help soon. If the heart space and emotional feelings of love open for your patient and that person says, "I think I love you," here's what I say:

"I am very happy for you that those old (such & such) feelings released. What you are feeling now is your own ability to love again. Feeling those feelings here with me, now, means that you are able to feel again and offer your deepest feelings of love to someone. Now you can live life with your heart open and look for that someone who will be able to return your love. I cannot, as my love already belongs to someone. But I am honored by your trust and the opportunity to have been able to help."

Honoring yourself and your patient means maintaining the relationship of patient and therapist. This allows you to continue to be the therapist and the patient to continue to heal and move forward. Awareness means a recognition of the situation of a therapeutic session. Responsibility means you— and only you—are responsible for maintaining the healing space for the patient. Trust yourself as the therapist that you have made a commitment to the patient to be their therapist (nothing else). Keep true to these boundaries of the therapeutic session. The patient's inner wisdom will recognize this in you and allow the patient to make core changes in your presence.

So the lesson from the session:

CranioSacral Therapy is intimate space where core issues are felt and influenced by intentional energy and compassionate touch. As Suzanne says, "It means facilitating a healing therapy session while honoring your boundaries and the boundaries of the client."

The great Native American flute player R. Carlos Nakai has a quote in one of his CD liners that he lives by. It strikes a cord in my heart, so I leave you with it.

*"To be of service to others,
I must be centered within my own awareness,
personal responsibility and self-reliance."*

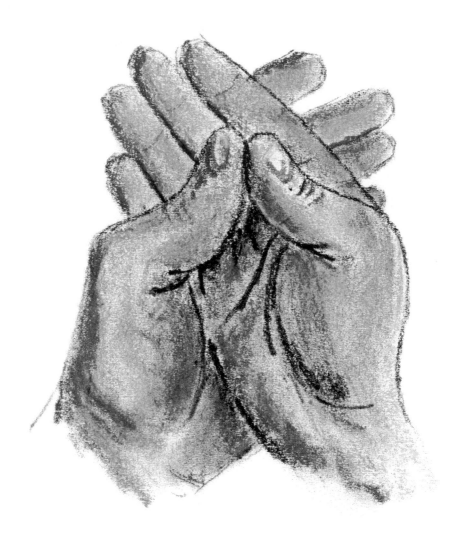

# 14

# Composing Points of Stillness

/have heard Winston Marshalis, the great jazz musician say, "If it wasn't for the silence and space between the notes, music would just be noise."

I have thought about that a long time and truly the pause between each noise of a musical note gives each note context, emphasis, unity, symmetry, measure, length, and composition. If all the instruments in an orchestra began immediately together, there would be a great, unorganized din of sound that could only be appreciated by bigness or volume. One hears that as the musicians enter a music hall and tune their instruments and warm up.

Is that what is happening to our culture? Is that what's happening to my time, my schedule, and my life? I find I am working harder, faster, and in more ways than I have in almost any other time in my life. Sometimes my life feels like a din with no space between activities. If I didn't love what I do, and build in still points to my life, I don't think I would be happy, healthy, or able to continue.

There was a time in my life when I was director of rehab services in a small hospital and beginning a physical therapy private practice in the early evenings, seeing patients in their homes. I was a columnist for a local newspaper, Chairman of the school board, and a volunteer fireman. I was a sheep farmer and trying to be somebody's father and husband, all at the same time. I was appreciating life by bigness or volume. But the volume of my activities, without points of stillness, was virtually killing me. I came down with gallbladder disease, mononucleosis, and double pneumonia—all within a year. Somewhere in one of those sleepless nights, when I couldn't lie down because I couldn't breath, my body brought me to a point of stillness.

A little voice said, "You need to change your life, or you're going home." I now know if it hadn't been for that point of stillness in the middle of the night, I wouldn't be here now. I have come to know stillness is very important in my life. It gives context, emphasis, unity, symmetry, measure, length, and composition. Now my activities are punctuated by periods of stillness. Sometimes it's Tai Chi in the morning, playing my flute, a midday power nap, or simply sitting in my kayak watching the sun come up or go down.

I am still learning about points of stillness. Did you notice that I still have to do something or go somewhere to get to stillness in my life? The most important part about silence between two musical notes is that there is no sound, and the most important part of stillness is being, not doing. We are human beings, not human doings. Being still means not being active. You are a musical instrument, but during a point of stillness, there is no sound. If I'm a saxophone in a band and don't play a stanza, it doesn't mean I'm not a saxophone. I'm still one hell of a horn. Causing oneself to be still requires that there be no doing, only being, no doing in the body or the mind. For the body, it means rest. For the mind, it means awareness. It continues to mean you are.

The challenge of our culture is to somehow find a peaceful way through all the distractions. If we can't do that, our lives lose their context, emphasis, unity, symmetry, measure of length, and composition. In other words, we are all business ("busyness"). We lose context in knowing whether we are human beings or employees. We only emphasize doing. We always have to be doing something. We have no symmetry, measure, or composition in our life between work, rest, and play. We don't know how we fit or what place we have in the world. Is it any wonder our lives have abbreviated length with an abundance of chronic pain, illness, suffering and less joy. We even lose the context of pleasure so that we have to purchase artificial replacement in synthetic substances or activities.

What pleasure stillness is! The schedule stops. Activities cease. The body can rest. The mind can pause. The spirit can come up and play. Too "muchness" and biggie sized everything can melt away for a time. In beingness, the spaciousness, quiet, and the sky-like nature of mind can move toward pure awareness and stillness. We can regain our context and composition. The way to stillness requires giving up doing. There are methods (okay a little doing) that can bring us to stillness. Sometimes repeating a soft pattern with the body can bring one to stillness: the gentle movements of Tai Chi, watching one's breath, or walking with the wind, simply resting on the activity of placing one foot after the other.

One method that I think has merit for the body and mind is CranioSacral Therapy. It requires that you intentionally lie down and stop your body. You also intentionally recruit another person to gently bring your inner body (CranioSacral Rhythm) to a stillpoint.

There are two major ways stoppage of the rhythm occurs in CST. One is that the body may seize the blessed opportunity to be gently touched in a safe environment, and go into a spontaneous stop. In this instance, resistance and hyper vigilance in the body may suddenly change. Body tone and awareness can instantly shift and physical release can occur. Release can take many forms, including: heat, pulsing, softening and spreading, breath change, digestive tract noise, eyes fluttering, and muscle fasciculation's—to name a few. We call this spontaneous stop a Significance Detector, because often an image, feeling, or situation, is brought to mind. Sometimes a traumatic or emotional recall comes into awareness. Often the body will take on the position it was in when trauma occurred. Traumatic energy from an energy cyst uses these moments to exit as well. This is a wonderful little epiphany moment for the person to recognize the emotional energy, thought pattern, and the associated quality of physical tone in the body. With dialogue, the rhythm can stop and start as a mechanism of communication, by the Inner Physician (see Chapter 24), to yes/no questions by the therapist. In this way Significance Detectors are stillness moments when both physical and emotional issues are processed by the patient.

A second type of CSR stoppage is a therapist-induced stillpoint. Based on the format of the listening stations, the characteristics of CranioSacral Rhythm, and a very gentle manual pressure, the therapist brings the rhythm to a stop. This is an intentional pause in the patient's body and mind. It is a silent space in the music of their lives. Releases and awareness that occur in a Significance Detector can happen here as well. As the body recognizes the rhythm has stopped, it automatically tries to restart it, and concurrently releases restrictions in the rhythm that were there before the therapist came along. In this way, new freedom and greater efficiency occurs in the system. Once the therapist recognizes the patient is in a stillpoint, he/she just monitors the changes and occasionally aid the patient in becoming aware of the changes that are occurring.

Here then is this pause, this silence, this beingness, in which one can explore one's true nature of awareness. This is a unique opportunity in our culture to remove the distractions of our daily lives, listen to our bodies, and release restrictions. Our lives can find meaning, joy, happiness, and rhythm. Understanding context, emphasis, and measure of experiences in our lives may help us compose a life worth singing. And isn't it learning "that everyone has a song to sing" what this life is all about? Composing points of stillness with and for the patient is one of the healthiest gifts one person can give another.

# 15

# The Sound of Sinus

*I* had two patients recently teach me about sound and the body. I'd like to recall the experience for you now.

You know sometimes the more you study something the more questions you create. As I continue to study anatomy I have asked very respectable anatomists from across the country what the purpose is for sinuses in the bones of the cranium. The most common answer is that the authorities are not sure. Some say they are there to collect infection when it erupts so that it is removed from the more central contents of the head. Others say the cavities of the bones make the bones less dense and therefore makes the head lighter.

Well, I am sorry, but I just can't buy that. Real estate is too expensive in the cranium to have empty lots all around. And we are talking about more than one bone and paired sinuses in each. Maxilla, Ethmoid, Frontal, and Sphenoid are the bones Gray states as having sinuses. I would offer up another candidate, namely the Temporal bones for its tympanic cavity, which is the superior end of the Eustachian tube.

The reason I include the Temporal bones and the Tympanic cavity is because of the nature of that cavity. It is here, in the inner workings of the ear that we receive the very broad spectrum of stimulation called sound. I wonder if the sinuses or cavities are there to receive vibrational energy such as sound?

I had an 85-year old opera singer tell me that sound makes the brain work better because sound vibrates the bones of the head. He had me place my tongue on the roof of my mouth and hum. He had me vary my intonations moving, as simply as I could, up my humming scale. In a low-ranged tone hum, I could feel my mandible and the back of my throat vibrate. In mid range I could feel my maxilla, cheeks, eyes and nose. And as I went to the high point of my scale I felt it most in and above my eyebrows in the frontal bone area. He said humming always helped him relax, sleep better, and discharge stress whenever he felt it. I really don't know why I am surprised by that. We have used high frequency ultrasound to hasten metabolism and for healing musculoskeletal injuries since the 1960s.

When I practice humming, it is healthy in many ways. There is the breathwork of it so one expands and evens out the lungs with in and out breath. There is the physical vibration of it as well. What a simple physical therapy and exercise. And as it relates to us in CST, it seems like a nice way to gently mobilize many sutures of the cranium. Is this why people hum, whistle, sing, yodel, or play flutes; to vibrate their head?????

The nature of the hum is steeped in ancient tradition. All Hindu philosophy emphasizes the chant called OM. OM covers the whole universe. This syllable is said to contain all the sounds naturally. AUM, according to rules of Sanskrit grammar, becomes the sound OM. This sound is used in every language by young and old to convey emphasis. "Oh my." "Oh no!" "Oh my God!" Hebrew, Arab, and English prayers end with "Amen," which when stretched out, said slowly, is AUM, or OM. OM is said to bring relief from pain for the sick, and expresses moods in the form of sound that in turn can bring peace and harmony. (*Complete Illustrated Book of Yoga*) by Swami Vishundevananda, Bell Publishing, NY, NY.

Another patient of mine recently gave me further insight indirectly as we were dialoging with pituitary. I was attempting to release some old trauma from a head injury and soliciting help from pituitary to activate the patient's endocrine system. Pituitary said she needed to rock and that I should do the techniques to facilitate that. I did frontal, parietal, and temporals and then from the sphenoid compression decompression handhold, I gently nudged the rhythm each way as I felt it from greater wings of sphenoid and occiput. She said she felt much better. As we were coming to the end of the session, I asked pituitary about the nature of the cavities in her bone (Sphenoid).

She said that all the bony cavities in the bones of my patient's head were there to pick up echoes. The high frequency sound vibrations make the organs and nerves of the brain work better. She went on to say that it helps her produce the several specialized hormones she is responsible for. The maxilla and ethmoid sinuses help the nose and facilitate smell. The frontal assist the reception and assimilation of light in the posterior superior orbits of the eye.

I replied, "Gee it must be difficult when they aren't full of air, but full of mucus during an infection." "No," she responded, "on the contrary, the density of the fluid adds to the migration of the sound vibrations, just like being in water. In this way, it promotes healing and activates the immune response." As I think of it, that must be why whales and dolphins have such large sinuses in their rostrums, to conduct and interpret vibrational sound transmitted through the water.

Not long ago CNN had a report about a Russian aquarium that was used to train dolphins to plant bombs on the underside of ships. (Nice use for dolphins huh?) Anyway, after the Soviet Union collapsed, the dolphins remained at the aquarium. They were then used as amusement for school children bused in from other areas.

There was an account of a group of hearing impaired children that visited the aquarium. After a short time the children all seemed to be excited and hyperactive in response to the high-pitched (tic, tic, tic) sounds the dolphins were making. The children's teachers were concerned and had them tested when they returned to school. Health officials found all the hearing impaired children, on average, had a 50% improvement in hearing from that one-day contact with the vibrational intonations from the dolphins.

I believe the more aware we become as a species in our receptive nature, our evolution will continue. Science is evolving into the notion that on a subatomic level we are all energy. Particle behavior is coming to be understood as being influenced by consciousness energy. Since energy cannot be created or destroyed, only changed in form, maybe we are at the dawn of humanity when we have sight, sound, taste, feel, smell, and we are all about to become aware of vibration. Could the spaces created in our heads by the sinuses be accessed and used as amplifiers for vibrational energy? Much like the sonar capacities of dolphins and whales, can we recognize—and cultivate for our own metabolic health and neurochemical production and circulation, the amplified echo vibrations in the inner chambers called sinuses?

Maybe that's why music is so universally acceptable and therapeutic. The Mozart Effect has been known to settle hyperactive children. And classical music has increased milk production in cows. I had classical music playing in my sheep barn during lambing time. I can attest to my own varying mood swings with Rap versus Jazz when my children were at home.

I asked the pituitary if it would be a good idea as homework for the patient to hum during her personal time in bed, in the bath, and in the car. Pituitary said yes indeed, and that she needs to rock and vibrate to function optimally. The patient has since reported a relaxing feeling and an increased desire to hum every chance she gets.

Lesson from the session: Empower your patients with self-help techniques they can utilize all their lives. Precautions, contraindications, and expenses are all zero. As it relates to brain organ health, this is a humdinger of an idea for your patients.

# 16

# Braille Bodywork

So, CranioSacral Therapy is for the visually impaired? Oh! So, it helps people who are visually impaired? You are visually impaired and this is what you do? No? You are not visually impaired, but you have invented a special language in which the visually impaired can see? Is that right? Is anything of this correct? Do you need to be visually impaired to do this work?

The purpose of this chapter is to explore the idea that CST is a form of bodywork largely dependent on touch, much like Braille. I am not talking about those that are visually impaired, whether that means 10%, 50%, or totally impaired. I am talking about bodywork that does not require visual sight. I would like to "catch the eye" of those that are visually impaired, but I want to address my thoughts to anyone that has the sense of touch. In this work we see with our hands. You may be visually or hearing impaired or paralyzed to some degree. You may have lost a limb or been through other trauma that may make you think you are unable to be a body worker. You may be a new CST student and question whether you can feel the rhythm or do this work. This is for you.

With CST (CranioSacral Therapy) we listen to the gentle rhythm of the exchange of Cerebrospinal Fluid (CSF) that prompts the health of the central nervous system and the whole body. We gently and lovingly encourage the body to change, sometimes with less than 5 grams of manual force. Sometimes it is important to recess one's vision, which is to look within rather than watching the outside of the body, the room you are in, or looking out the window. What I mean to say is, we—as CranioSacral Therapists—listen to the body, look within with our hands, and ask the body to change. We have a technique known as the Upledger 10-Step, in which we release musculoskeletal and connective tissues associated with structural and functional tensions. Then there is the SER (SomatoEmotional Release) process, in which we listen to the body in terms of its CranioSacral Rhythm and the stoppage of the same. We then dialogue with what stopped the rhythm. Sometimes it is ego, fear, sadness, guilt, shame, or anger. Sometimes it is memory of traumatic pain, tension, body position, or other emotions that may accompany an event.

As the work relates to release or the therapeutic effect, in no account of the work or the attributes of the release—either physical or emotional—does it declare that one requires physical, visual sight. Matter of fact, this is a work in which the sense of touch is cultivated. One is encouraged to get out of the head and into the hands. Frequently the best practitioners occasionally close their eyes while feeling the patient so that their eyesight is not a distraction to their cranial rhythm listening potential. In an effort to facilitate optimal progress for the patient, the therapist extradites him/herself from the current physical environment, and focuses on being present exclusively with the patient during the session.

This does not mean that all CranioSacral Therapy should be done with the eyes closed. How the patient stands, sits, walks, holds their head, and lies on the table, offer visual cues about tone and structure. One is wise to use all the tools available, including vision. But, having done that, or should vision not be available, it isn't essential. And, in the overall picture, the cultivated sense of touch is far more important for this work.

I have had my eyes closed and watched a rhythm come to a still point. Sometimes as a patient relates to me what they are seeing with their eyes closed, I can see with my imagination what they are seeing. I recess my vision, or pull it inward and try to see with my hands. It is a form of perception that can help the therapist feel release in the patient's body in forms like heat, pulse, and the rising of physical or emotional energy.

A very subtle awareness that has helped me, is closing my eyes as I evaluate the cranial vault. From the head of the table, with my hands in the first vault hold position (lateral position), I close my eyes and visualize the circumference of the head from the superior aspect. I look with recessed vision to see an energy glow around the head circumference. It looks like a thick circular strand of fuzzy yarn. As I focus on it, I can often see a burst of energy, light—or excess yarn, if you will—coming from a portion of that circle. Asking the patient where the problem is, they will often describe pain coming from the exact spot on my loop of yarn, conforming to the pain spot on their head. During reevaluation after the session, I often find that the abnormality in the energy loop is changed, diminished, or abolished.

A very useful application to recessing vision is with temporal bones. First, we use our visual cues and tactile sense to land our finger placement accurately on zygomatic arch proximal to ear, external auditory meatus, and the mastoid process. Then as we monitor CS rhythm, we gently take it out of synchrony by holding one temporal bone and allow the other to move within the rhythm to the opposite extreme. As that is achieved, we simply ride them, now out of synchrony, one moving anterior, one posterior, still within the confines of the rhythm. We then nudge each (5 grams). In this technique (circumduction, or finger in the ear), I have found it extremely useful to have my eyes closed. I can just be my hands and ride the rhythm from the temporal bones. I "watch" them move anterior and posterior with my hands. Sometimes as I ride these bones, it feels awkward and I realize they are already out of synchrony. I am better able to notice this when my eyes are closed.

As they move to extremes of range, one anterior, one posterior, still within the rhythm, it affords me an opportunity to put them in still point—one anterior, one posterior. I find after still point occurs, I am better able to perceive rhythm return with my eyes closed. This is the case for me with CV4 as well.

As a visually impaired person constructs letters, numbers, and words from varying dots and spaces, a competent practitioner can compose an image of the patient by feel. We focus on the rhythmic pulse, arcing for energy patterns and/or other tissue restrictions and variable release signs, along with the verbal processing of the patient.

So, is CST Braille bodywork? In a way it is. Cultivating the sense of touch allows us to see with our hands. To blend and trust, and allow time to be our ally, and to focus intention; these are the elements common to reading Braille and doing the bodywork of CranioSacral Therapy.

Is it easy to learn Braille and CST? In the few times I have tried to identify letters in Braille, I found it very difficult. In my first CST seminar I left on the fourth day thinking I may have felt something that afternoon, going through the many positions of the 10-Step. I know now that most things worth doing are not easy to learn. Mahatma Gandhi said, "If I have the belief I can do it, I shall surely acquire the capacity to do it, even if I may not have it at the beginning."

The lesson from the session today: To those of you who think you cannot feel cranial rhythm because you lack the ability; keep trying. CST is much like Braille. It is a beautiful communication system that will enrich your life and open you to a world of new possibilities and insights.

# 17

# Be A Bridge

*H*ad a patient's mom call me one Friday afternoon, frantic that her 21-year-old daughter was in severe pain in the left wrist, shoulder, and neck.

She was an aide for a summer school program that included special needs children. Apparently an eleven-year-old girl became agitated and when our patient tried to calm her down, the eleven-year-old grabbed our patient's first two fingers and hyper extended them, then twisted them, causing her arm to flex at the elbow and twist behind her back. The student had an emotional outburst and began yelling at our patient, who was by this time on her knees, in pain, and also yelling—but for help. The student was removed with the help of another teacher.

Our patient went to the hospital for x-rays, then to an orthopedist who said nothing was broken, but there may be some ligament damage. He put her in a wrist splint and an arm sling. He told her to call in a couple of weeks for a re-evaluation. He also gave her pain medication.

Her mother called the doctor the following day saying her daughter was in excruciating pain and would the doctor see her again.

The doctor said no, there was nothing he could do, that the level of pain was all in her head, probably psychosomatic, and she was going to have to live with it and get over it. Both mom and daughter were former patients of mine, and mom in her desperation called me that Friday afternoon.

I could tell by the sound of her voice that she was alarmed, upset, and at a loss as to what to do to help her daughter. I had them come in that Friday afternoon at 5:00 p.m.

She presented with splinted posture, (holding her arm and leaning forward.) I had her lie supine with one pillow under her head. After listening to her rhythm I did thoracic intlet, hyoid and her right arm began to twitch. I moved to her arm and held it from the palm and elbow. It abducted from her side, and then extended down below the side of the table. (If the table wasn't there I have a feeling it would have curled behind her back.)

She began to remember the assault, and said she felt fear, pain, and then began to cry. There was heat and pulsing from the arm and regional tissue release, as it moved slowly at the side of the table. This situation continued for 10–15 minutes, and then subsided.

The patient sat up remarkably relaxed and relieved of 80% of her arm and neck pain. Both mom and patient were very relieved but then became surprised at what I then said to them.

I said, "You know, that orthopedist was exactly right. I think your problem was largely psychosomatic. We call what just happened to you a SomatoEmotional Release. Sometimes when trauma happens and the physical strain and stress is placed in soft tissue, the emotions, at the moment of the trauma, get placed there too. Bad stuff happens to good people. That is what happened to you. The doctor you went to is a good doctor, but he is a surgeon type of doctor. He fixes bones when they break. He knew what happened; he just didn't know how to help because no bones were broken.

Treatment was followed up two more times and included range of motion exercises. She went back to the M.D. after two weeks, told the doctor what happened and he said, "I'm glad things worked out."

The lesson from the session here is that basically we need to remember we are at a place in history in which there is currently a huge paradigm shift.

That is, we are moving from a 100-year allopathic medical model of anesthetizing the pain until it goes away, or cutting it out surgically. Technology has made physicians strain to comprehend new pharmaceuticals and the interactions at the rate of 40,000 new chemical combinations per year. Surgical advances in computer-enhanced radiography and robotic surgery have made most physicians at least part-time students—just to remain current and updated. To assume the allopathic physician then has the luxury of a working knowledge of integrative medicine is, at best, a stretch.

As integrative practitioners, I think we need to be a bridge — helping the patients cross the barriers to holistic healthcare, as well as acting as an avenue to constructive change that for some allopathic physicians is a vast canyon, the crossing of which seems most unnatural to their left brain footings.

We need to treat all allopathic physicians with patience and co-exist by example, as they heal, grow, learn and move onward in their own very human lives. They are trying to keep up with technical change as paradigm change is washing away some of their foundational thoughts.

Biological, chemical, and mechanical process is no longer absolutely repeatable and replicated in double blind study. The notion of spirit, energy, energy transfer and quantum physics renders the scientific model as we know it increasingly obsolete.

We need a new model based on clinical trial, objective findings, and results-oriented treatment outcomes with human subjects. I urge my colleagues in CST to support their local MDs, DOs, DCs, other practitioners, and patients in this wonderful time of change, as they struggle to understand what we are doing.

# 18

## Trade

*I* had a wonderful old patient a long time ago who taught me about Trade. He was an independent old German by the name of Rudolph. He and his wife came to this country after the war (WWII). He was a shortwave radio operator who assisted the French and Allies by intercepting and translating German radio messages. When they came to the United States he had a strong German accent and a continuing interest in shortwave radio. He bought a modest home but had a large shortwave antenna on the roof. During the fifties and the McCarthy era, he was questioned about his radio activities. Some folks in our conservative rural New England town thought he was a communist spy.

Rudolph paid particular attention to being part of the community. He went into town every Tuesday to trade. He had a small war pension and also a settlement from a local factory where he was injured in an electrical accident that left him with one-sided weakness, a drop foot deformity, and neuropathy of one arm and shoulder. He also had lost his right eye and wore a black eyepatch. Mothers would gather their small children near as the big man passed by with his broad-billed hat and long, dark coat—a limp as he walked and his black-patched eye.

I asked him one time why he called going to the store trading. He said that's what they called it in the old country. Once a week his family would go to town and do their trading. They would use their hard earned money and trade it for goods they needed. They bought food, medicine, clothing, and visited with their neighbors in the various shops. Merchants would earn money to trade for goods they needed, and the community would spread money around for services to each other, and in this way rural towns prospered. Sometimes money wasn't involved at all. Farmers sometimes traded eggs or produce for coal or shoes or cloth to make clothing. Doctors back then commonly accepted chickens or cordwood as payment for medical treatment. Rudolph once said he traded the chickadees sunflower seeds in the winter for their company. He showed me a picture his wife had taken of him and a little chickadee sitting on the brim of his black hat.

So how do we trade for our services? Some of us are employees. We work in hospitals, clinics, or for an owner of a practice; and we are paid either by salary or by the hour from our employers. Some of us are paid by third party—that is, insurance companies charge the patient money (usually, a lot of money) and when the patient needs services, the insurance company pays the provider money (usually less than the provider asks for). Some of us still trade directly with the consumer for our service. They come, receive treatment, and trade by paying money for the service.

Here in New Hampshire some of us trade in ways other than money.

1.  **Trade:** the business of distribution, selling and exchange any kind of business, to make an exchange with someone, to exchange or barter. *

2.  **Exchange:** the giving or receiving of one thing in return for something else. *

3.  **Barter:** to exchange goods or services against something else without using money. *

---

*Laraouse Illustrated International Encyclopedia and Dictionary.*

I've provided physical therapy services (which in the last decade or more has been CrainioSocral Therapy services) for a variety of items in trade. I have traded for equal time on the table as a patient myself. I have traded sessions with my teachers as a student, with my students as a teacher, and with colleagues. It's a wonderful way to share and stay healthy myself. I've traded for a knitted afghan and pillow. I've traded for an old utility trailer. I've traded for one oil and one pastel painting. My most interesting trade was with a farmer friend of mine. I traded one day's work with a bulldozer clearing my woodlot road. Another time I traded for manure. I had worked all winter with a family member of his. In the spring he called and asked me about payment. I said my wife was just starting up her garden center and could use some manure out in the field where she was planning her show gardens. He said OK, he'd bring a few loads over.

I went back to work seeing patients all day and had forgotten about that early morning call. As I said goodbye to my 3 o'clock patient at the back door, we both could smell something "funny." I followed the scent out my door, down the ramp and between the old farmhouse and the barn, out toward the field.

There in the field lay a dinosaur in repose. I couldn't believe my eyes. I had a long pile of manure, six or eight feet high, ten to twelve feet wide, and over fifty feet long. Marty was just pulling out after the last load. "Marty, Marty, we're paid in full man," I said. He smiled and said he'd brought four loads in all. I asked him how much manure was in one truckload. He said about 20 yards. One yard of anything is 3 feet, by 3 feet, by 3 feet. Well, 20 x 3 is 60, and 60 x 4 is 240. If you can imagine seeing 240 one-yard square blocks of anything stacked in a tall, wide, long pile—that's what I was looking at. This was fresh as a daisy, right out of the barnyard, still steaming manure. We both smiled and went on our way.

So how much should we charge for services? Just because CST is wonderful and sometimes helps patients better than a half a dozen treatments of some other kind, please don't charge $250.00 per visit. Charge what the fair value is for your time and service.

I'm reminded to say here that much of the therapeutic gains are done by the patient, the patient's body, and the Inner Physician. With significant and unusual sessions you, as practitioner, learn as much about treating people as the patient receives in health benefit. There have been sessions in which I felt so honored to be present that I simply couldn't charge anything.

Lesson from the Session here is; remember you are part of your community. The service provided is of value equal to others' service in your community. We live and work together. We trade our skill, time, and service so that we all may prosper.

Be like Rudolph and be a part of your local community. Providing CranioSocral Therapy as we do, we are likely to stand out in the crowd and be questioned. Like Rudolph, be true to yourself, tell the truth and be fair in your trade. Trade for equal measure whether it be money, service, or manure.

# 19

# One in Singapore

Sometimes it strikes me that I really am blessed. I mean, not only do I love what I do, but I have the unique opportunity of offering it to the world.

I have traveled twice to Southeast Asia for the Upledger Institute in the last five years. The first time was in March 2002. It was the first time for an Upledger class in Singapore. Kqueen, a wonderful lady, whose family has historical significance in Singapore, sponsored the class. During the Japanese invasion in the early 1900's Kqueen's uncle was part of the resistance and a leader for independence. He and others were captured and tortured, and a statue raised in their memory is in the national park.

For many years Singapore was a British colony and the original British hotel, Raffles, is still famous for their Singapore sling. Singapore Is an Island nation with diverse culture, composed of Indian, Mala, and Chinese populations. People born in Singapore are very proud and are culturally rich in Asian heritage and also English influence.

As I came to this country I was totally outside anything that was familiar. Remember now, I'm from New Hampshire, USA. We'd had snow on the ground for the past five months; commonly sub freezing temperatures, and a barren winter landscape.

I arrive, after 24 hours in three different airplanes, to a tropical paradise. On the last leg of my trip, I remember, I was gazing out of the airplane window. It was a bright star-lit night. As we approached the coast of Singapore, there were hundreds of tiny single lights below the plane. It was surreal trying to distinguish the moonlit starry sky from the small fishing boats in the ocean below. The sky and ocean merged into one in the moonlight. It was as if I were traveling into outer space, to some great faraway beyond. I was on the "Star Ship Enterprise" and about to explore a new world.

Singapore is amazing. It is a paradise with wondrous plant life and a humid, tropical climate. It is a young country with well-educated, youthful street crowds—well dressed, well informed, and worldly in their eagerness to prosper and build their country. Central avenues in the city are like Times Square, New York. The sides of buildings are huge T.V. screens, full of motion and color—advertising everything from politics to pop stars to clothes, food, and the services of this most modern, high tech metropolitan world venue.

Coming from New Hampshire, and a hands-on natural healthcare rural setting, I was out of my element. I was the only Caucasian to be found in most places other than an occasional Australian tourist. All the buildings were flat roofed and pastel colored in every shade. All the apartments were multi story and nearly every window had a long flagpole for drying clothes. The tall buildings were a wave of brightly colored personal clothing drying in the sunny breeze. Street signs were in kilometers, Chinese and English. All the people were foreign to me (a very rare experience in my life). All the vegetation was strange with orchids and bright flowers draping from canopy shade trees on roadways, parks, walkways, and public transportation entrances. Even the birds in the parks were foreign to me. The train system was beautiful, clean, and color-coded for easy access. Being a former British Colony, most people spoke exceptionally excellent English. Most of the food was unfamiliar. We had frogs' legs, rice, lots of vegetables, fish, stingray and prawn (shrimp), and lots of tea. Singapore has excellent beer called Tiger Beer, which I explored thoroughly when dining out.

With all these new dimensions to every facet of my existence—from doorbells outside each hotel room to orchids, multi-colored birds and foreign streets and people—I was awash in new experiences. I awoke every day, grateful to be alive and wondering what newness awaited me. It was a new and wonderful adventure every moment as an American tourist.

But then, I wasn't there on holiday. It was my privilege and challenge to teach the first CranioSacral Therapy class ever in Singapore. And this was my great lesson and the reason for this writing. What I found familiar—in an otherwise totally new, foreign, and exotic world—was the Cranial rhythm. It dawned on me the second day of class that people are the same the world over. As I ventured out in the streets, used public transportation, ate and then taught, listened, questioned and interacted, I learned we all are the same. We are one. Singapore young therapists are trying to blend traditional medicine with the allopathic model of the west. They have trouble the first time using their hands and listening to the rhythm just like in the states. There is commercialism, materialism, chauvinism, and prejudice—just like in the states. There is the social stress of drugs, alcohol, relationships, and climbing the corporate ladder—just like in the states. There is pain, tension, injury, abuse, violence. There is also hope, love, pride, honor, courage, bravery, kindness, compassion, and desire for peace and happiness—just like in the states.

Cranial rhythm, listening stations, energy cysts, direction of energy, stillpoints, SomatoEmotional Release, and physical and emotional releases are all universal. They have the same effect here. They are as common, and as essential, useful, therapeutic, and personally profound as they are at home. People are as inquisitive, energetic, lazy, ignorant, selfish, conceited, egotistic, and loving, kind, considerate, and eager to learn and grow—as any of us.

Lesson from the session is that we are all one family. We all have insecurities, strengths, skills, hopes, fears, loves, and we are all eager to live in the pursuit of happiness. CranioSacral Therapy is universal and not some current fad of our western culture. It is important, giving, self-empowering healthcare that has merit in cultures from sea to shining sea. SomatoEmotional Release is universal in matters of fear and love and emotional release and bridges Muslim, Hindu, Bahi, and Christian beliefs.

As personal journeys go, you can learn Upledger CST, jump off a plane, land on an Island, push two tables together in a corner café, and live happily ever after.

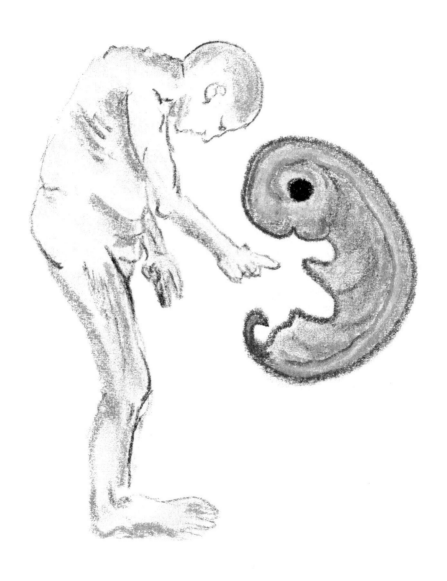

# 20

# Generations In Hand

*I* got a call a few weeks ago from a former student. She said she needed a session and so did her nephew, and she wondered if I had remembered her. She was the one that had a SomatoEmotional Release about her and her baby after class one day. It was back in 1999. When she said her and her baby, I had instant recall.

"Oh yeah, I remember," I said. It was one of the most memorable sessions I had ever had....

She had taken the CSTI class about six or seven months after giving birth. She was a medical professional with over four years of medical training and had a practice, as well as a young family. She was really enthusiastic about CST and very much wanted to add it to her rural practice. She also had sacral and pelvic pain since giving birth and was hoping to find something that would help her. As it happened—I think it was after the second day—she came up to me after class saying some work by another student appeared to have caused more discomfort in her lower back and pelvis.

As is often the case, as we learn elements of the work, old pains and memories of pain sometimes surface. I make a particular effort to ask students how they are feeling each morning during Q&A. It is good to talk about little aches and pains as they come up because this is typically what can happen with patients. Students need to know this is part of the patient's process and not a function of improperly performed CST. (Although that can happen on occasion as well.)

When on the road teaching—and I think I can speak for most teachers when I say this—we really put forth a lot of energy teaching each day's material. At the end of the day, we are tired. A favorite teacher of mine says he has just enough energy to push the up button (on the elevator). So, it's not a time to volunteer to treat anybody. One doesn't have enough energy to stay present and attentive to a patient on the table. Besides, if you treat one "somebody" then everybody will want to be treated. It's also good to remind yourself, and anyone asking you to treat them, that you really can't, as you (likely) are not licensed to treat in the state you are lecturing in. I, or my assistants, will offer some students who feel out of balance, spacey, or strange-feeling to take a moment or two and do a CV4 to help ground them so they can feel more relaxed traveling home.

On that second day, while I was packing up my things there were two TA's on a table exchanging CV4s, and this student came up to me and asked if I couldn't do a still point on her sacrum as she felt sore after another student had done her. I ended that day of CSTI with a CV4 lecture and demo, so I said sure, I'd do a sacral still point.

As it often happens, serendipity (as Dr. John puts it) seems to be alive and well. Things have a way of happening for a reason. I told her to lie down and I went to the hand position for the pelvic diaphragm to get a sense of what was happening. I like to listen to the rhythm from this position, although it is a fascial release position.

She went into an immediate still point. She was a stand out student. She asked great questions those first two days. She came with her mother, who was babysitting her infant daughter. The grandmother would walk in the hallway outside the classroom. Sometimes we'd hear the baby cry and my student would have to leave the class for a few minutes to breast-feed. So, in still point at the pelvis, I asked her what she was thinking. She immediately folded her knees, turned on her side, and began to cry. I knew then that this was going to be more than a still point induction.

"I'm thinking about my delivery. It was horrible."

"What do you mean?" I followed.

In tears now, she recalled how guilty she felt. She had had a home delivery. She had gone into labor and was fully dilated, but the midwife hadn't arrived. She tried not to push but the baby really wanted to come out. She was angry with the midwife and afraid to deliver alone. She placed three fingers on the crowning head of the baby keeping it from being delivered. She held this posture for over 20 minutes, until the midwife finally arrived.

Once the midwife arrived, the delivery was fast and relatively normal from that point on. But the mom has felt guilt about restraining the birth and the feeling that there was an incomplete connection between her and her infant daughter. She felt that her daughter must have thought her mother hadn't wanted her to be born. She has harbored guilt and negative feelings in her lower back and pelvis ever since.

I asked her if she wanted to get rid of those feelings. She said yes. I asked her how and she said she didn't know, but the surges of pain came in waves, almost like contractions. I then asked her if she wanted to deliver these negative feelings out of her like giving birth. She agreed and rapidly thereafter, with the slow, gentle, gradual pressure of my hands on her abdomen and lower back, she began visualizing her feelings of guilt about her daughter's birth. She said she could visualize and feel those feelings being evacuated from her pelvis through her vagina. Just as this was happening, I heard her (actual) baby crying in the hallway, and as I looked up, I saw Grandma holding the infant in the lighted doorway. I motioned her to bring the baby in.

I asked the student if she would like to hold her new baby without the guilt of thinking she had stopped the natural birthing process. She gave out an emphatic yes! I took the baby from Grandma and placed her in the arms of her mother, still lying on her side. She held her baby close to her chest as if it were just born. The baby stopped crying, and the three of us adults began to cry. There was a sacred quiet moment as we all witnessed a new and changed relationship between mother and child. Mom later reported all pelvic and back pain abolished and her relationship with her daughter was altered in that her baby was more inclined to be hugged and held than ever before.

My gratitude for the opportunity to be a witness to a relationship change between mother and child of such profound and dramatic proportions has remained vivid in my mind to this day.

So when this student called, I had this vivid recall and curiosity about how she would present. We arranged an appointment. The session began with talking. She sat on the table and said she had developed anger toward her stepbrother. She said it was very difficult in their living circumstances. She and her husband own a large house and have two young children, ages 3 and 5. Her mother and father live there as well for several weeks at a time, as her father travels often to her region for work. Her parents adopted her stepbrother two years ago. The child, now 13 years old, had been mistreated and beaten in infancy. Since coming to live with her mother, the boy has frequent outbursts of temper and is very disrespectful towards adults—her mother in particular. She went on to relate how she sees her mom straining to care for this boy; being emotionally hurt and becoming physically drained. She feels angry and jealous that her mom has no time or energy to be a grandmother to her children. She also does not want her children to learn or mimic her stepbrother's misbehavior. She also relates that she is 14 weeks pregnant and she fears her present feelings would somehow interrupt what she hopes will be a happy gestation period.

By way of CST, we found a restriction in her upper abdomen. We utilized visualization and journeyed down her spine where we found a tight, heavy band of anger going from the pancreas to her left hip. She wasn't able to remove the band, but by way of intention, she was able to change it to a soft white cord of "tolerance." She then continued down her spine and became upset, saying she felt dead below the waist and she couldn't get in touch with her uterus. We looked and she found that she had built a huge cinder block wall up between that band of anger and her uterus in order to shield the uterus and the baby from the negativity of those feelings. I asked if she still needed to do that now. She paused, looked inside, thought, and said, no, it was no longer necessary. Block by block she broke down the wall and moved further caudally toward the uterus.

She continued her mental imaging down to her uterus and again she became anxious. She said she saw a large black blob covering part of her uterus. She wasn't sure what it was, but was sure she didn't want it there. For good resolution, I knew it was very important to find out more about it.

So I said, "Would it be okay if we asked your uterus what it is."

She agreed and with her permission, we engaged uterus. Uterus was not hesitant to respond. Uterus said the blob was shame. Uterus said she felt shame being pregnant when the host was angry. She (uterus) felt the anger was directed toward her for becoming full with a new fetus. I explained to uterus (with patient's permission) where the anger had come from and that it was not directed towards her and was no longer there. Uterus was happy about that and said she no longer had to be so tight and that we could remove the black blob. It looked like a heavy oil slug that sometimes forms a round blob in the sand on the beach. It covered approximately one quarter of the patient's pear shaped uterus. With gentle encouragement, the patient was able to slowly, gently, roll it, like a thin rubbery film, up and off the wall of the uterus. Patient was happy, uterus was happy, and I was in awe (and happy). I asked the patient and uterus if they wanted to re-place shame with something else. They both said, "Love." So, we spent several minutes sending and surrounding uterus with love. It was a sacred place now.

We slowly moved our way back up the spine. The patient had presented this day with a deep cough that caused me to almost see her bronchial tree lurch and restrict with each deep hacking cough. On our way back up the spine, I said, "Would you like to look at your lungs while we're right here?" She said, "Yes," and I continued, "Do you know what is causing your lungs to feel con-gested?"

She hesitated about two seconds and said, "I'm exhausted, worrying about my pregnancy, my kids, my mom, my stepbrother."

"But," I said, "you don't have to worry about your pregnancy now, you are connected with your pelvis and you have transformed your anger to tolerance. Do you really need to continue to ex-pend this excess energy and become exhausted."

"No, I don't have to worry so much now." She paused.

We spent several more minutes quietly. My hands were in the thoracic inlet position. She got quiet again and then she gave a large full breath. (A classic breath change release.) She said that was the first full breath she had taken without coughing in a week. We then continued back up the spine and into her head from where we started and the session was complete. She had tears of relief and completion as she sat up, taking slow, full breaths.

"I wonder what would have happened to this baby and my uterus if I hadn't done that," she said, staring out the window with one hand on her chest, the other on her pelvis.

Neither of us will ever know. I do know this; sessions that ex-plore core emotional and physical holdings can effect lives that haven't really begun yet. Sometimes the work can resolve issues between generations and help to heal the wounds that have been ongoing for several generations. We have generations in hand as we help people find understanding of themselves and relationships in their lives. I am often struck by the patient's sudden realization of some lost truth. At those little epiphany moments, emotions in the body relinquish their hypervigilance and the tissues of the body change tone. The emotions, the mind, and the spirit then take on a new demeanor. It is in these quiet moments, after a long session, that I am reminded of the writings of Carlos Castaneda in which Don Juan says:

"For me there is only the traveling on paths that have heart, on any path that may have heart. There I travel, and the only worthwhile challenge is to traverse its full length."

"And there I travel, looking, looking breathlessly."

---

* *Since the time of this writing the patient came full term and delivered her baby at home with the support of her family and midwife. The grandmom told me recently that the experience was loving, natural and all she and her daughter had hoped it would be.*

# Part IV

## Lessons in Inner Wisdom

# 21

# Best Friend

From time to time we all develop friends and friendships. We come to a time or circumstance when we can embrace and trust another without question. There is faith enough for us to rest in a space without doubt that there is one true friend who would never hurt us and would always want what is best for us. That true best friend would look upon our happiness and successes as their own. That faithful friend would never fail to stand by us in times of crisis, pain, grief, and loss. That special one we could depend on, would be there to share our sorrow and suffering, as if it were their own. That one wonderful, solid soul would stand by us, and even try to carry us to safety and out of harm's way. At their own sacrifice, and to the possible detriment of their own safety, they would protect us, and try to save us, to the very end.

What is a best friend!!? Who is your best friend??? Although my outer best friend is my life partner Jill, my inner best friend is the one I am inextricably connected to. My inner best friend is my body. I believe your body is your vehicle to move through this life with, but much more than that. There is an inner consciousness in all the structures—from the large organs like the heart, lungs and liver,—to the smaller ones like pineal and pituitary glands. And smaller yet are specific types of cells like lymphocytes, stem cells, and protein molecules.

As we consciously talk to ourselves each day, (and I know I do), who is it that we talk to?

Thoughts:    I didn't sleep well last night!
I better go to bed early tonight!
Maybe I won't go to that meeting tomorrow night?
Why can't I sleep anyway?
What is the matter with me?

If you had one true friend who was with you all the time and always looking out for you, but who is unable to talk directly to you, how would that friend get your attention?

Let's say you were out at a party and having a great time and you stopped counting how many drinks you had because you were feeling good and it didn't matter. Without knowing it, the alcohol level in your bloodstream became so high your liver was getting backed up. You had been drinking for over eight hours, urinated a lot, and began to become dehydrated. The dehydration caused a decrease in the amount of cerebral spinal fluid going to and circulating around your central nervous system and brain. Your mental functions were beginning to wane. Vision was distorted, balance was precarious and verbal wording was beginning to slur. Your Reticular Alarm System was so relaxed, you no longer anticipated danger, like traffic in the road or the subway train approaching. Your stomach lining was becoming inflamed by all the alcohol passing through it.

What would your dear friend do? First thing he does is give you the hiccups to wake you up and make bringing a glass to your mouth difficult. Then he gives you a headache which makes you not want to party anymore. Then he makes you dry in the mouth so that the ice cubes begin to taste better than the drink. Then as you start to move and go outside in the air your wonderful body initiates a gag reflex. You evacuate your polluted stomach contents of alcohol, pizza crust, tomato sauce, and petrified salami chunks into someone's prized peony show garden and cobblestone walkway. Your other comrades witness your miserable condition, recognize you can't drive, so they carry you to the basement and let your body put you to sleep under the pool table. Your Body Friend saved your life.

You're playing basketball and trying extra hard to play like you did 10 years ago, when you were in college. You make your old signature move to go around somebody. You twist your out of shape lower leg and ankle and fall to the floor. Teammates joke and say, "Hey, what's the matter, can't you play like you used to?"

You start to get up, "I'll show you I can still play!" But in an electrical bolt of instant intense pain, you look down and grab your ankle.

Words come immediately to mind, "Damn, I can't play. Look at my foot and ankle. It's swollen bigger than my head. And it is hot. I can't walk on that. I'll have to elevate it to make the swelling go down. I'll put some ice on it to get rid of the heat, and make the pain stop."

See, your wonderful Body Friend did that. Body Friend gave you those symptoms so you wouldn't hurt yourself. The pain and swelling would make you rest so as not to hurt your leg further. And from the bench you may now realize you can't play like you used to. (An enlightenment of no small favor to your safety in the future).

Our great inner Best Friend tries to contact us by whatever means necessary to move us away from an unhealthy environment, substance, or circumstance. This is the nature of the inner voice of the body. That is why rotten food and its putrid smell repel us. Pain stops us from putting our fingers in the fan. Immobility and pain may be the best escape into rest and quiet, from the stress-filled, pressurized, multitask, material world that is consuming our bodies.

Lesson from the session here is that our bodies may not be falling apart as symptoms erupt. Symptoms are signals from our Best Friend to pay attention. Bringing your patients to quiet points of stillness may allow them to listen to their Best Friend, and make changes in their lives to return them to health and happiness. This is facilitating healing of the highest order.

# 22

# The Land of I Got

$E$nergy work as part of the paradigm of health care remains a nebulous business. There has been energy work in medicine since there has been medicine. Witness hot, cold, electricity, ultrasound, ultraviolet light, x-ray, MRI as examples. My friend Jim Oschman has written a wonderful collection of historical references of energy and medicine. (*Energy Medicine, the Scientific Basis*)

Some effects of energy in medicine are physical. Some are sometimes not so physical, but with a physical or physiologic result. These effects range from change in muscle tone, pain and circulation modulation, chakra intensity, synchronicity and alignment, SomatoEmotional Release, and simply a change of mind.

The first energy shift is from the patient. A person feels pain or feels an obvious lump that was not there before. The person feels afraid and worries that the unpleasant sensation of pain won't stop or the lump is some harbinger of great illness, sickness, or death. This energy shift raises feelings of fear, apprehension, self-consciousness, and a degree of concern—and even panic in many people, which is also an energy effect. One's personal safety and physical continuance is called into question.

The next energy shift is toward relief. The person subjugates him/herself into the form of "patient" and seeks something to quell the symptoms. They may apply ice or heat or simply rest. They may seek services of a doctor for medication, an injection, or surgery. They may even seek the services of an Integrated Medical Practitioner. The method the patient chooses is the next very important shift. There is the sense of trust and hope that the method will work. So the patient imparts faith in the process.

That's one of the reasons for the huge rise in holistic medicine. Patients have lost faith in medications when they read the ever growing lists of side effects and complicated, dangerous drug interactions that accompany prescription drugs. Faith is important. Whatever else faith may be, it is the conscious intent that is a mental energetic activity at least, and a spiritual and/or cosmic connection at most, to be called forth or otherwise employed to serve. This part of the process needs to happen for optimal health because we as human subjects know it needs to happen because of our evolving neocortex. I'm sorry doctor, but we are simply more aware than we were in the 1950s. The hippies started it in the 60s. This is why we, as a current population, are more in tune with our bodies. This is why dealing with emotions, feelings, and self-intuition is the new and important paradigm for body workers like physical therapists, occupational therapists and massage therapists in helping to improve physical function.

Another very important and new paradigm change in medicine is that the provider must also enter an energy shift. Allopathic model did not require this. The therapist just administered the method or treatment and simply attended to the consistency of delivery. Here in this energy-aware holistic model the therapist blends with the patient and tries to feel what is going on in the body. What happens in each body is different in each body. The therapist must be open and aware of the varied reactions a patient can have to relatively standard treatment. Standardizing feelings is like standardizing pain response. It has not been done yet to the satisfaction of Newtonian Scientific model. This energy model requires faith and trust, and the ability to change on the part of the patient and the therapist.

When the patient seeks help from a healthcare provider, I feel it is the responsibility of the provider to assist the subject by paying attention to how the body presents. I also feel we do a disservice if we project our feelings, values, or interpretations into the process (in a way that artificially influences the subject and the subject's body).

How does all this relate to energy work? Sometimes the healthcare provider gets a feeling or an awareness that may or may not belong to the patient. I've seen manual therapists put their hands on a person's heart and feel all kinds of energy coming out. They look, listen, feel, and say, "I *got* a sense of shame here. What are you ashamed of?"

The therapist has just injected the notion of shame into the patient's process where it may not have been. If the therapist is wrong, he/she just made a mistake. But for the patient in process, understanding of what is happening within their body may just have been tainted—thrown into question—and pushed off process and away from the single-minded concentration needed for healing.

I've had this happen to me. I was gently holding a patient behind the head in the occipital cranial base position and I could feel heat and pulsing. This went on for some minutes, then "I *got*" a sense of pain and fear. I thought about what I was feeling and it continued, causing me to silently ask myself, "Maybe I am applying too much force? Maybe I've held this position too long? Maybe I shouldn't be doing this with this patient?

Luckily, I didn't voice what "I *got*" from the patient—to the patient. Feelings of panic and fear continued and then they shifted and changed. They became less intense and the patient's neck began to move and unwind. It suddenly occurred to me that this must be a part of the patient's process, not mine. I held this position (because of what I got) and this therapeutic period of time afforded the patient's body an opportunity to gently release a musculoskeletal component of holding and restriction, apparently caused by emotion. The patient remained silent and voiced no complaint about my hand pressure or what was happening.

Then, I said to the patient, "What are you feeling now?"

He said, "Funny you should ask just now. I am feeling fear. It's just like the accident. I felt the same fear when I heard the ambulance but couldn't move my head or raise my arms to signal for help."

If I had said, "Do you feel shame, anger, sadness, or fear?" or something else, I may have interrupted a wonderfully orchestrated release from this person's body. I know many experienced therapists often feel emotions or energies coming from the body. Many, many times the therapist is accurate in recognizing a sense of energy corresponding to an emotion. Medical intuitives specialize in recognizing energy emitted from the body as having common effects. A certain energy sensation is known as coming from the liver, or the way a body is shaking is always an indication of anxiety, etc. Often a medical intuitive session will end with a consultation.

The patient asks, "What do you think?"

The intuitive may say, "Well, I *got* that your heart is unhappy. It's about your mother. I *got* that it is very old. I *got* the sense that it's preventing your heart from working right, and this is why you have neck and left shoulder pain."

Therapeutic points are lost if you, the therapist, make discoveries for the patient. You, the *manual therapist*, shouldn't be the one to "get things." It's the patient who needs to "get it." The patient may or may not have an emotional component to their pain complaint. They may or may not have a relationship problem with their mother. You may feel a feeling that occurred in your heart when you had a relationship problem with your mother. The smallest loss of concentration opens the door for this type of transference.

So, what is a manual therapist to do when they sense something important that they feel the patient needs to know? The first thing that is important is to allow ample time for each session. This is particularly important with SomatoEmotional Release. (See Upledger) If you only have 15 or 20 minutes it might be best to stay structural with your intention and direction of energy. Simply intend to encourage physical releases only; and not an emotional release that may need lots more time to process.

If you have the time, (60–90 minutes) by far the most constructive tool I know to bring forward genuine patient emotion and feelings (if they are there!) is to ask very neutral questions. "How are you feeling now?" "What are you thinking?" "Do you feel anything happening between my hands?" Each question needs moments to several minutes for patient contemplation and quiet-time assisted self-assessment.

If the patient feels some change in their body, continue with neutral questions—the answers will produce more concise awareness of images for the patient. Such a response may be, with their eyes closed, "There is a dark thing in my back."

Confirmation that this is significant in their process is always accompanied by a spontaneous stop in the cranial rhythm. We call this a significance detector. (See Upledger) That is the reason we, as manual therapists, have business in this mind/body process of the patient in the first place. This is the essence of how CranioSacral Therapy facilitates the patient's process.

Leave plenty of time to answer, but your questions may include, "Oh really, what shape is it?" "What color is it?" "What is the temperature of it?" "Have you ever seen it before?" "When?" "Where?" "How old were you when you saw it for the first time?" "Is there more than one?" "How does it make you feel?" "Does it need to be there?" Exploring these images allows an opportunity for understanding, and thereby growth and change.

Here is where SomatoEmotional Release and facilitated dialogue really begin. (See *SomatoEmotional Release & Beyond* by Upledger.) The therapist and patient now have an image (identified by the patient) to work with. The therapist may initiate dialogue by asking the patient,

"If you don't know what that dark thing is, would it be all right if I tried to talk to it?"

"Okay, I guess so," is often the response from the patient.

Therapist follows, "Would it be okay if that dark thing used your voice to talk to me, and would you let it say whatever it wanted without sensor or judgment?"

"Okay...sounds weird, but I'll try it." is a typical response from the patient.

There we go on a dialogue with dark thing using neutral but encouraging questions,

"Hey dark thing, it's Don (patient's name)'s therapist. You must be real important for (name of patient). Would you come and talk to me for a minute so we can understand why you are here?"

Dark thing may be a current emotional holding. It may be an energy cyst in a joint or muscle group. It may be a spinal subluxation or a facilitated segment. It may be an old emotional holding from a family relationship. It may be the body's attempt to get the attention of the owner.

The bottom line and the lesson from the session is: What it means to you (the therapist) is not as important as what it means to the patient. Allow the patient the opportunity of self-discovery. Once an image comes to their awareness and an understanding of their illness occurs, the patient can relax, rest, exercise, and finally heal. They can look at the issue and deal with it now, or not. Be careful and be aware of your use of the words "I Got." Use I *got* information as insight in order to pose the most neutral questions to facilitate the patient's process. Let the patient "get" what you "got" in his or her own way. They will then own their own discovery and recovery. And you will be the simple little facilitator you were meant to be.

# 23

# OCB The Great One

*I* usually come to day four of the CSTI class discussing clinical applications, and someone always asks me what is the most important step in the 10-Step Protocol.

And of course I say, "I don't know." How could I know? Every Cranial Rhythm, like every human, like every dural tube and brain, is unique and has different features and special needs. I have read and heard on tapes many authors say that the CV4 technique is the one in which a therapist acts locally, but treats globally as it relates to impacting the craniosacral system in a comprehensive way.

I'd like to generate a discussion and offer that OCB (Occipital Cranial Base) is the great one. Here are my thoughts.

The Occiptal Cranial Base is a great transitional place in anatomy. It is as great as the confluence of Sinuses at the Internal Occipital Protuberance, and Sutherland's Straight Sinus Fulcrum. It is where the Menninges transition from a large spherical structure with cross membranes to a linear tubular structure. The attachments of those membranes at the foramen magnum are the most inferior for the cranial vault, and most superior for the dural tube.

Biochemically and ergonomically the area of C1 and occiput are vital to survival. Witness the most common and ancient form of execution—hanging—which fractures the odontoid process

(Dens) residing in the area of C1 and occiput. A loss of integrity here means the flow of the river of life stops.

The Cranial Base is the pivotal place that suspends the 8–12 pound head upon the body. Considering our bodies are mobile units with arms, legs and locomotion, head and neck stability are vital to navigating space, speed, and timing. This part of the body is also the conduit for our airway, feeding tube, and blood supply to the head, not to mention the total central nerve pathways of the body.

The body in its wisdom has surrounded the area of OCB with extensive muscular and ligamental support, from the large upper fibers of the Trapezius and Sternocleidomastoid to the very intrinsic Rectus Capitus Posterior Major and Minor and the ligamentum Nuchea. Scaleni, posterior, hyoidal muscles anterior provide other layers of support.

The potential for compromise and injury in this part of the body is huge. Who has not had neck strain, whiplash, muscle tension headaches, referring arm pain, weakness, and parethsias; personally or with clients, patients, and family members?

Our culture is replete with references to the neck. A goodly portion of the national debt could be abated if all the necklaces made of gold, silver, diamonds, and jewels that hung around our necks were sold. Adornments occur in every culture and include all manner of neckties, collars, lapels, and fine cloth ruffles created of fur and linen. The value of this part of the body is clear.

The release of tension, tone, and restriction in this area completes the diaphragm release techniques of Upledger's 2nd step of the 10-Step Protocol. And it is the entreé to the other techniques of the fabulous cranium. Hand placement and quality of touch here often sets the stage (or not) for change in the head.

Upledger divided this technique into four parts. The first is the platform. Both hands are together at the 5th digit and lateral palms. Fingers are together and perpendicular to the palms. Finger pads are on the inferior margin of the occiput and fingertips are in the space between C1 and occiput. This isn't an easy technique to master as we have the entire weight of the patients head on our fingers, just subsequent to initiation of 5 grams of traction. I'm reminded here to say that the optimal patient position is flat on the air mattress, but acute symptoms and/or extremes of age may require modification with pillows and/or partial weight on thenar and hypothenar areas of the palms.

Contraindications are rare in CST, but there are some. Systemic disease such as cancer or osteoarthritis where the vertebral body integrity is compromised would be a contraindication. But remember this type of patient is probably not walking. Disease is so severe the vertebral body is simply squashing like a sponge. And of course any condition in which increase in circulation in the cranium is detrimental is a contraindication for this work in general.

Injury or dysfunction of the cranal base is usually a case of the occiput being abnormally anterior of C1. Our fingertips are gently influencing the posterior aspect of C1 and encouraging cervical musculature and connective tissue to soften, spread, and allow C1 to gently reposition itself anterior in relation to occiput. Mechanically, as this happens, the therapist can feel the weight of the head gently express itself into the palms. The head tips back and the therapist's fingers curl slightly in order to maintain contact with the finger pads on the posterior ridge of occiput.

Once this event has occurred, we move to the next important aspect of the technique. Postition the first and/or second fingers (depending on your hand and finger size) on the large transverse process of C1 thereby creating a stabilized landmark from which the therapist gently begins slow, superior traction at occiput. This distracts occiput from C1. Third and/or fourth and fifth fingers gently traction occiput superior from the anchored transverse process of C1. Two points here. First it frees up restrictions of occiput and C1 so that we can, in the end, traction the dural tube from the next major attachment site, namely C2 and C3. When trauma occurs, typically C1 facets medically influence the occiput condyles. This can restrict the foramen magnum, and the contents that pass through the foramen.

After having tractioned occiput from C1, we simply spread the condyles of occiput with the fingers we just used to traction it from C1(commonly 4th and 5th digits.) It's a slow gentle one-time spread that usually takes 10 to 20 seconds. Remember this part of the technique is important to free the cranial nerves 9,10, and 11. The vagus nerve is so global in influence, this step is really wonderful for the body.

We now arrive at the wonderful moment of having released tissue anteriorly, superiorly, and laterally. With all of these dimensions liberated, we now have the opportunity to traction the dural tube and continue to influence the vagus nerve as well as the entire dural tube. Remember, where we are in the 10-Step process. We have, just a few diaphragms before, tractioned the dural tube from L5-S1. Now we explore traction from the superior aspect of the tube.

For my money this is the best feeling technique there is. Upper back muscles relax. The gapping of that space (C1, occiput) and gentle traction is liberating to my exiting nerve roots throughout the cervical spine. My neck, head, arms, and whole body just soften. As in Greek Mythology, the weight of the world is lifted from the shoulders of Atlas.

The lessons I have learned from here makes it really obvious to me how great OCB is.

I know I have helped the patient at least come to a place of partial relaxation. I know I have arrived at the gateway to the cranium. If I stay where I am at the cranial base and continue my gentle traction, I can envision the dural tube. Sometimes segment by segment—a muscle or muscle group on one side by muscle group on the other—restrictions gently give way. Sometimes this causes slow undulating regional tissue release from the muscles of the neck. You can see twitching of an ankle or feel searing heat at occiput. This is often the place where patients experience a sudden change in muscle tension or posture and they exclaim, "I can't believe I was holding my neck and shoulders so tight."

From this beautiful site where I have my hands, at the end of OCB, I can now monitor the rhythm. I can dialogue from here. I can fascial glide the body from here. Much of the work with infants by way of modified technique can be done from the sacrum and here. I can very respectfully exit and draw a session to a close from here. It is from here that great things can happen for the patient. Is OCB the best technique of the 10-Step Protocol? I don't know, but it is a great one!

# 24

# Guidance

*I* consulted a person I trust on this one. As one journeys with people, speaking to them on the table, and with your hands, monitoring the rhythm; there comes a certain guidance.

John Upledger has explored the subject beyond any other person I know. He has devoted his life to the work of being guided by the patient to reflect back to the patient what he/she needs to know to live happier and healthier. He has shown people their way on the path of their lives. He has done that through CST, which has encouraged physical releases from the body. But more fundamentally, and at the essential core of living, he has aided people who lie on his table, and enable them to identify and form a living, working relationship with their inner selves. There are many words to describe Inner Guidance. There is Inner Physician, consciousness, inner self, inner guide, and inner wisdom. There is conscience, sub-conscious, self-conscious, collective consciousness. There is inner child, higher self, and little birdie on my shoulder. And as we contemplate our own mortality there is God, Tao, Spirit, Soul, Holy Ghost, and Rigpa (space of unborn mind). Dr. Upledger has been able to access this awareness in a most generic and unique form for each patient that wants to explore it. He has identified this inner knowing and wisdom as simply the patient's Inner Physician. It is unique to each individual. There can be more than one Inner physician depending on need. It's like having a doctor, a dentist, and a psychologist. It is void of the trappings of religion, psychology, astrology or spirituality. It honors the patient's belief system and this life's constructs, in that it is the most accessible avenue to personal understanding for each patient.

That said, how does one find one's Inner Physician? Well, one has to ask, and one has to listen. In order to be able to ask, one has to know the right questions. And in order to listen, one needs to be quiet. Both qualities are hidden in our culture by mountains of trappings ranging from diagnosis, advice, over medication and surgical intervention to absurdly excessive busyness of materialism, ownership, socially tolerated drugs and endless temptations, and recreational distractions.

Interestingly, one of the few places one can get quiet and receive help in asking for and receiving acknowledgement of one's own generic inner guidance is on the CST table. I think one of the greatest goals of CST is introducing the patient to their inner guidance. This can come directly from the session or as an ongoing processing from work received on the table.

Inner Guides can come in many forms, from departed family, animals, natural things like trees or rocks. Inanimate objects can be precious guides like a white room, a black box, a window, a brick wall, or a doorknob. Sometimes the guide is a body part like the heart or pituitary. Depending on one's need at the time Inner Physicians can be transitory. For example, with severe, unrelenting neck or head pain that may have suddenly appeared, Upledger will bring the patient to stillpoint and ask for guidance from the head. When asked, cerebellum may announce itself by using the patient's voice and then proceed to offer advice on the cause and remedy for headaches. On another occasion in another session for a different problem, the same patient may be guided by the liver to solve a problem. Sometimes a recurrent guide like an animal, object, or a loved one will appear and direct the patient and therapist's attention to cerebellum, liver, or other body location. Communication can then more precisely and accurately cause change and healing in a specific portion of the body, whether it be physical or emotional healing that needs to take place.

One time my friend told me his story. He had been taking classes at the UI and treating people with CST. He had been receiving work himself, both on the table in the classes and in trade with fellow practitioners. My friend had begun to be open to the changes he was feeling. He had become aware of his own needs, for his body, mind, and spirit. He released tensions and visceral holdings from old surgery, trauma, and the stresses of daily life. But when asked in CST session, if there was someone inside who knows about this (i.e., injury, restriction, tension pattern), the answers would come but no guide would ever appear. Others had images and visions of guides. He longed for an inner vision and guide to speak to and receive from.

Even in his advanced class with Dr. John in Florida in 1990, he worked on people who saw amazing visions. Characters appeared to influence and change lives for his classmates. He had releases and SERs but his information came in non-verbal awareness and sudden bursts of knowing. They were authentic and wonderful but without author or known origin.

Time passed and then he began to have dreams of a large fierce animal chasing him and his family up a steep mountain grade. He and his family would tire of uphill running and collapse. He would turn, face the ferocious creature about to attack, and suddenly awaken and stop the dream. This dream came about once every 3–4 months. Then once a month, then once a week. Finally it was twice a week. His sleep was disrupted. He was becoming fatigued, irritable, and certainly tired of this sleep interruption. Finally he resolved to stop it. He told himself he would not end the dream as he had before. The next time he would see it through to the end and stop this constant irritation.

The appointed night and subsequent dream occurred. The animal appeared snarling, clashing its teeth, and ripping its paws through the air as it charged him and his family, as they once again fled uphill to the point of collapse. As they all stopped in breathless terror and exhaustion, he turned toward the charging animal. He had no stick, rock, or weapon. The animal rose up for one final lunge at him. He remained fearful but steadfast and determined to finish the dream. He drew his fist back, and with all his might threw an all-out-effort punch in the face of the oncoming monster.

What happened next left startling moments of disbelief, for he felt his heart race, his arm and shoulder recoil, and then explode in a passionate last defense of his imperiled family. To his total surprise, his fist met a soft cloud of cottony cushion, as if he had punched an eight-foot goose down pillow.

His surprise met an instantly recognizable intimate soft familiar embrace. The voice that had answered all his questions in all his CST and SER sessions for years, became instantly audible. The raised ferocious beast was gone and in its place sat a large creature with a gentle smile on its face. A moment passed, and understanding dawned and he saw and heard this great animal that now sat on his haunches like the old family dog in the kitchen. "Face your Fears."

The words, the pause, the transition of this mortal enemy to an old trusted friend, teacher, and guide sent waves of warm new thoughts and awareness gently lapping one after another upon the peaceful beach of his consciousness. Suddenly…finally…here was his guide. And surely as he had faced this most perilous situation he could face any situation in the remainder of his life. As suddenly as these thoughts moved through his consciousness filter the great animal spoke again.

"I will walk beside you, help you, guide you in the spirit world. I will always guard your back all the remaining days of your life."

He has since asked his guide for assistance in his sessions and as he treats others.

As he told me this story, he said I could retell the tale but not to mention what kind of animal or the animal's name. He said it wasn't secret, it was private—and in the Native American tradition, his personal guide is sacred and to be known intimately by only him and his closest family and friends.

Lesson from this session is that there is no need to try to find your guide. Your guide knows when, where, and how to contact you. Live your life as best you can, ask for guidance often and be available to listen in your quiet personal times when you are in your bed, out in nature, or on the table. Guidance is available, if you ask, wait, and listen…always!

# 25

## Trust Guides

*T*his patient who is in her early forties, has had major stress in the last two years, and has lost her hearing in her left ear since her divorce. She has had psychotherapy, currently sees a chiropractor, and in the past has had two sessions of CST with mouth work. She is a pleasant lady, looking younger than her age, with long blonde hair. By way of CST we recognized changes and tissue release at the sacrum, thoracic inlet, hyoid, OCB and then particularly, temporals (mastoid). She had neck and cervical muscle regional tissue release and then came to a still point, at which time she could feel her left ear tingling and she didn't know what that was about.

I asked her if she wanted to find out. "Okay," she responded. I then ask her, "Do you think there might be someone inside you that might know?" "Well I have two guides that I have been aware of but I've never spoken with or heard them speak. They really only appear in my dreams. One is an Indian, another is an old doctor by the name of Dr. Morton." (Names and genders may be altered to ensure confidentiality.) I ask, "Would it be okay if I tried to speak to one of your guides?" Again, she says okay. "Would it be all right if one of your guides used your voice to speak to us?" She paused and smiled and had a little hesitating laugh. "Well I guess it would be okay, I have never done this before."

"Which guide would you like to try and contact?" I ask.

"Dr. Morton I think."

"Okay.... Hello Dr. Morton. This is Don, Gloria's therapist. I would be greatly honored to speak to you for a few moments about Gloria." "Very well," came the response in a soft tone that was distinctly different than the patient's. "Have you been aware of Gloria's pain and loss of hearing in her left ear?" "Yes, she needs traction at C1&2 on the right."

(At this point, I had done OCB, frontal, parietals, temporal wobble, and then she had still point.) I said, "Thank you, if I put my hands on C1-2 will you guide me as to pressure and direction?" "Yes, I will be glad to," came the calm response. I placed my hands at OCB with slightly more pressure on the right than left. My hands were in a cupped position as in the 4th step of OCB. I began gentle gradual superior traction. Dr. Morgan initiated comments, "Press more lateral." I replied, "Like this?" (Doing like a lateral spread of the condyle on the right.) "Yes," he replied, "now traction upward." "Like this doctor?" I asked, as I tractioned superior. "Yes, quite correct, your intuition is right on," he said.

Gloria said, "My inner ear is tingling and with my eyes closed I can see a nerve coated with something." "Does that coating need to be there?" I asked. "No, I think it needs to come off." "Go ahead, with the hands of your mind's eye, see if you can scrape it off," I offered. When patients see something like that I tell them to pretend they have imaginary hands in their mind's eye. We then proceed inward and they remove anything from scar tissue to negative lumps of energy. There was a pause of several moments when Gloria said, "There, it's all off, it kind of flaked off."

"How do you feel Gloria?" I asked. "I think I can hear better now," she said.

I moved toward a closing, "Thank you, Dr. Morton, for helping us. Is there anything Gloria needs to do?" "Yes, she needs to consult with me more frequently, and apply ice." I said, "Gloria, did you hear that?" She smiled shyly and replied, "Yes, two other energy body workers have told me that." She forgot to tell me. "Hey Gloria," I quipped, "get with the program. This is an important, powerful guide for you." She smiled. Rhythm returned from my monitor at the OCB, and she opened her eyes and said, "Wow, that was awesome. I can hear and I don't have anymore pain." I applied ice to her neck for five minutes and finished with a brief massage.

Lessons from the sessions here is to trust your guides. Strongly encourage your patient to honor, listen to, and respect these insights. One of the most valuable awarenesses you can offer the patient is introducing them to their Inner Physician. Also important for the clinician here is to listen carefully to the Inner Guide—honor and comply precisely to the guide's directions, even if it seems repetitive, as it was in this case, having to redo OCB. There was a subtle traction moment I had missed. Repeating made all the difference for the patient. Interacting with the Inner Physician is also one of the most dynamic, spontaneous, and fascinating events for clinicians. I can't think of a more useful, efficient activity or modality we can do clinically.

# 26

# Never More Than One Can Handle

As a teacher of the first level course in CST, I have the wonderful privilege of ushering novice students into the CranioSacral system. Along the way and sometimes even in the first four days, one or more students experience a SomatoEmotional Release. Subsequently the question always arises "Suppose that happens to me with my patients?" "Suppose they freak out, crack up, or lose it? What am I going to do?"

My routine answer as part of the discussion includes the statement that the patient's system will never give them more than they can handle.

Recently that paradigm was tested in my office and it proved to be a lesson for all concerned.

A patient came to see me complaining of long-standing neck and shoulder pain. She had limited range of motion in the neck by 50% in all planes; and with any motion greater than 90° of shoulder flexion, she had tingling in her fingers. She was a receptionist and did heavy document filing that often required her to work at shoulder height and higher. She had no traumatic event that she was aware of, and stated that she had a low level of pain for years. Recently, (in the past six months) it had progressed and become worse. She had been through standard pain medication and physical therapy with no improvement. She came to me knowing that I did CST and that people with chronic pain sometimes had benefited.

We began with the standard listening stations and from the heels, I noticed multiple muscle fasciculation or twitching. Her neck gently turned slowly from side to side, and as it did one shoulder would rise slightly. She said she felt very strange and had a tentative smile and occasional giggle as a body part would move involuntarily. I told her that her body was using this session to release tensions, and I explained the characteristics of release and the benefits of decreasing hypertonicity in the muscles of her back, neck, and shoulders. She had several spontaneous still points, and when asked,  she had no reflection of an old injury or the rising of emotion or the awareness of a current issue in her life. She left feeling as if she had worked out and said she was tired. I told her she might feel more sore from all the motion she had experienced with her neck and shoulders, and maybe we would alternate our sessions of CST with a session of moist heat and massage. She left with another appointment at the end of the week.

As it happened, I left two days later to teach in Wisconsin. I left a list of my patients on our schedule board. My associate, a new grad P.T., experienced in techniques level CST, saw the patient on the following appointment. Apparently, she read my note about doing CST but not the part about using modalities at the next visit. I had placed the patient in the schedule at mid afternoon, thinking modalities would help her at that time in her workday. The patient said she needed to return to work after treatment.

So the patient came in and my colleague began the session with CST. The patient began as in my session with multiple regional tissue releases. But this time the releases kept going. The patient said she really had to go back to work. My colleague obliged by ending the session but asked her to at least sit for a few minutes, have a glass of water, and let her body settle down. The patient declined saying she'd be okay and really needed to get back to work.

She returned to work, but began to experience more trembling in her hand so she was unable to write or type. Her neck began to flex forward, and one leg began to flex at the hip and knee involuntarily, such that she could not sit or stand. The patient's co-workers became alarmed. She became alarmed. She contacted her doctor and he became alarmed, and referred her to the emergency room. There the E.R. staff became alarmed and gave her a Demerol injection. The involuntary motions continued. The attending physician sent the patient to radiology for a CT scan of the head. The physician called my colleague and said our patient was in some sort of possessed state and did she have recommendations? The patient was given another Demerol shot, and after two hours, her husband was called to bring her home, as her symptoms were quiescent. By the time she left the hospital, she'd had a brain scan, blood work, IV meds, and a psych eval.

She apparently was releasing more than her body could handle—or was she??? My colleague called me that night long distance relaying the situation. When I returned I found that the patient had called and scheduled another appointment with me. Furthermore, her husband, a former marine, would drive her to the appointment. He was not in favor of her return and would be in the session with her to ensure that what happened last time wouldn't happen this time. She was scheduled last in the day.

So, with that background, the patient, her husband and I arrived in my treatment room at the appointed time....

We began at the heels and again she began to have substantial regional tissue release at the neck and shoulders. The patient said, "Here we go again, what's going on? Why am I doing this?" Her husband sat on the edge of his chair with his hands on his knees. I said, "You know, your body is really trying to bring our attention to your neck. I am going to go there. I went to the thoracic inlet. I asked if she thought her neck might know what was going on. She didn't know. I asked if I could talk to her neck. I turned to her husband and said that sometimes the body really needs to express itself, and, I know it seems strange, but it may lead us to some understanding. I asked again and the patient said okay.

"Hello there Jill's neck, I'm Don, her therapist. It sure seems to me like you are trying to get our attention, is that right?"

"Yes," came a terse answer.

"You sound like a powerful Inner Physician for Jill, have you been in her a long time?

"Ten years."

Seems to me like you really have a need to move, have you needed to move like this for some time?"

"Yes it has been 10 years"

"Jill said she's had neck pain for years. Do you know how long she has had her neck pain?"

'Yes it has been 10 years."

"Gees neck, did something happen to Jill about 10 years ago that started all this?"

"Yeah, he was mean, he was rough with her, he would have really hurt her if I hadn't stepped in and held her neck and shoulders stiff. I've had to hold them ever since."

At this point, my ability to dialogue was superseded by my perceived awareness of Jill's husband leaning forward on the edge of his chair with his hands on his knees. He sat behind me, about three feet. Was the patient loosing control of her body? Was the source of her obvious negative contact present in the room only inches from me? What should I do now?

Sometimes what you think is happening is what is happening and sometimes it is not. You really have to blend and trust the body and the process. I came back to the dialogue. I elected to Blend, Trust, and continue.

"Hey neck, can you tell me exactly what happened 10 years ago to begin your holding and tightening?"

"She went to the dentist. He pulled four teeth. He leaned down on her jaw with all his weight. He pulled and twisted. She was in pain and stiff and sore and worried about getting back to work."

At this point, I wanted to check on the awareness of this event with Jill. "Hey Jill, are you hearing this conversation?"

"Yes, she said, "I remember that now. Oh my, he was really rough— my neck and jaw were so sore. I was out of work for a week. I had headaches, felt dizzy and I couldn't go to work, remember?" she replied, directing the last question to her husband. He remembered.

I then went back to the neck, "Well neck, can we work a deal here? If I just support Jill's head and you let out all that motion you have been holding, will you stop holding?"

"I don't know, I have been wanting to move for so long but I can't let go!"

"Why can't you let go?"

"Because sometimes she gets tense and nervous and that's how it started with the dentist."

"Do you hear that Jill, your neck seems to think you get tense and nervous lately."

"Well, we've been so busy at work. I mean, I really like my job but sometimes there is so much to do, so much filing before I go home."

"Jill do you think if you relaxed a little at work that your neck wouldn't have to stay so tight?"

"I guess so."

I followed as her neck began rotating and turning, sometimes flexing towards her chest bringing her to a sitting position. Gradually over a period of 10–15 minutes, the movements became very slow and subtle, and finally subsided.

"Neck," I asked, "how about a deal? If I have you and Jill come in once a week and we give you all the time you need to let go of your holding will you save your movements for then and not do them other times, especially when Jill is working?"

"Okay I can do that."

"Is that okay with you Jill?"

"Yes it is, that would be great. People at work will be happy about that too. They were really worried about me."

Did this body give the patient more than she could handle?

I think the body recognized the opportunity to release and took advantage of it. Unfortunately for all concerned, the patient's work schedule (requiring her to return to work) did not meet the needs of the Inner Physician.

Lessons from the session here are several:

Colleagues, take the necessary time to read your colleague's notes thoroughly. It might make the therapeutic experience go a little smoother.

The Inner Physician can read the skill level of the therapist; time available per session; and facilitate the appropriate amount of release. Lesson from the session here is also for the therapist to set the stage for the work, so that it can fit the busy lives of all of us.

With the appropriate dialogue, perimeters can be negotiated to allow the Inner Physician to do the work it needs to do, without making the patient unable to function.

Example:

"Okay, Jill, we'll start our session now. Take all the time you need in the next 50 minutes to encourage your body to release before you go back to work."

As I continue to do this work, I am constantly taught lessons and methods to help the patient. And I am ever learning the wonderful, powerful inner abilities of the body to experience the adventure of CranioSacral Therapy.

# 27

# Sutherland Lives

$\mathcal{S}$ometimes when we contemplate Inner Guides we think of some entity that is maybe spiritually majestic, like an angel or a lion, or a buffalo. There are Inner Wisdoms that take on peculiar forms, sometimes a box or a ball. Often we hear Inner Physician names that are historically significant, like Gabriel, Gaia, or Socrates. But sometimes Inner Physician names are not famous or beautiful sounding. They can be named Ralph, Henry, or Cowboy Bob. There are occasions when the Inner Guide is so common an entity that unless one remains impartial, one might not respect or honor the advice given.

I recently was working with a 54 year old female. She presented with a ten-year history of back pain from a lifting injury. Her history also includes an anomalie in her lower lumbar spine with a sacralization of L-5. She came to me for evaluation and said she and her M.D. were considering surgery.

By way of listening and multiple still points she came to an awareness of heat, pulsing in her lower legs and "funny feelings" in her legs. At thoracic inlet, she came to a spontaneous still point. Her eyes were closed and I asked her what she was thinking. She volunteered that a little old man with white hair came into her vision.

"Does he have a name?" I asked. "No," she said, "he won't speak...." There was a pause. "He's grumpy. His arms are folded and he is just looking at us." "Well, would it be all right if I tried to talk to him?" I followed. "I guess so," she ventured, "but I don't think he'll speak."

And sure enough, he didn't. After the usual prerequisites, I asked if we could honor him by knowing his name. He must be a powerful guide, and we sure could use his help. Would he be willing to show us where to go? I waited, she waited, and we waited.

Then she said, "You know, now I am getting a sharp pain in my back, down low and also in my left knee." I moved my hands to the pelvic diaphragm. Then she said, "He's pulling on my neck and spine. I think Grumpy wants you to pull on my tailbone."

I knew she was connecting with this grumpy little white-haired man so I took her vision as my non-verbal orders from the old man. I gently switched my hands and went into L5-S1. As I could feel the sacrum gently migrate inferiorly. I asked, "Is this what you want me to do Grumpy?" She said, "He is nodding his head."

We did this for several minutes until I felt the sacrum unable to go further towards her feet. I got a repelling feeling, so I asked her. "How's Grumpy doing, is he still pulling your neck?" "...He's slowly letting up," she followed. I knew she was still connected to him and watching him intently.

"Where do you want me to go now, Grumpy?" I asked.

She answered, "He wants you at my neck." So I slowly moved to the head of the table and thought he must want me to stretch her spine from the occiput. So I began the platform position for occipital cranial base.

Then she said, "No that's not it. I don't think you have it quite right. He said something strange to me. I think he said, 'Tell him to bathe the brain.'" She had a questioning look on her face. "What a strange thing for him to say, what does that mean?"

Well, I sat straight up and brought my head back and looked in disbelief at her, contemplating what I just heard. All this patient knew of CranioSacral work is what I had told her. I flashed back to W.G. Sutherland's book, *Contributions of Thought*. In that book he often referred to CV4 as being the technique that could influence the entire central nervous system, that it would literally "Bathe the Brain" in the river of life—the cerebrospinal fluid. This was common verbiage in early cranial work but not for a neophyte patient to come up with on her own. I suddenly recalled the back cover of Sutherland's book showing the gentle little old white-haired man holding a skull in his hands. And I know our very own John Upledger has mentioned that phrase "bathe the brain." I then changed from OCB platform to CV4 and did 3–4 induced still points and I could feel her neck relax, then her body soften. I rested in confidence, she would make great progress from this point onward, and she did.

Lesson from the session here is: Just because the Inner Physician you encounter isn't a Greek God or a majestic eagle, doesn't mean the wisdom conveyed isn't powerful and important. Listen to the patient's guide, even if it is a grumpy little old white-haired man, 'cause you never know who you are going to meet. Nice talking to you, Doctor.

P.S. Because of the way I was aided from her Inner Guide, I am of the opinion that the Osteopathic world may be softening to the idea of therapists doing CranioSacral Therapy.

# 28

# War Goes On

*I*'ve heard it said that history repeats itself. That came home to me strongly the other day. I asked the patient if I could tell his story. I said I would change names and circumstances slightly to protect his privacy. He said I had his permission to tell it exactly as he had told it to me. I'd like to share with you now.

P. presented in my office complaining of pain in his left shoulder that was of six months duration. He is sixty years old and relates no injury, accident, or traumatic event. His referring physician cleared him of any cardiac history. He also complained of headaches that began after a fall from a ladder many years ago, and related a long history of intermittent low back pain and nervous leg syndrome at night. In addition, he takes Zolof for depression and anxiety that he has experienced for more than 10 years.

As a physical therapist specializing in CranioSacral Therapy, I was cognizant of his diagnosis of left shoulder pain. But with his history and his multiple pain complaints, I was going to view him as a whole person. His body was working hard trying to tell him something. As people come to me, I say to them that they have tried conventional medicine, now I would like them to try something new. I would like to gently hold them, listen to their body, and go where it leads and wait for releases. Once I talk to them about the central nervous system, the production of CSF, and

177

how tissue and emotions inhibit CSF production, they seem willing to try the experience of a session.

So, that's how we began as P. was lying on my table and I began to listen from his feet. I soon got up to the upper chest and shoulders, at which time the cranial rhythm stopped. I asked him what he was thinking.

He said he was concerned about the recent news of the war that had just begun with Iraq. He said the pictures on T.V. were bringing up old issues he had about war. I asked him if there was any one issue that came immediately to mind.

He said he was a Vietnam Vet and during that war, he was a crew chief in charge of the maintenance of fighter planes. He viewed his position as one of responsibility for both his planes and his fighter pilots. He always had a question of doubt about the death of one pilot and whether he was at fault or whether he could have done anything to prevent the pilot's death.

He said he went to Washington D.C. a couple of years ago. He wanted to see the Vietnam Memorial. It was his first time and it really struck him, particularly after he located the name of his special pilot on the wall. He was standing back from the wall in silence, just reflecting quietly. He was the only one there as it was a dark rainy day. Suddenly two young children running ahead of their parents came to the wall and looked as if they were searching for a name. He watched them and they came to the name of his pilot. There they placed a strip of paper on the wall and with a pencil rubbed his name on the paper.

The parents had caught up to the children by this time and P. just couldn't keep from approaching the people to ask about the name they had copied. The mother gathered the children protectively from this big city stranger, but the children's father answered. He said he was a cousin killed in the war. P. said he knew him too, as he was the pilot's crew chief.

Everyone was suddenly struck with surprise at this coincidence that the only two groups of people at the monument were both there for the same person. As I write this I can see and hear John Upledger smile and remind me that there are no coincidences, Don! The people there exchanged phone numbers and P. was invited and encouraged to call the pilot's mother, which he has done a couple of times since.

With P. still in stillpoint on my table I asked him if he'd like to learn more about the pilot. He answered yes. With his permission, I asked his Inner Physician to assist us in learning more about the pilot and his plane. We asked P. to close his eyes and try to see the pilot. He smiled and had a little tear in his eye. He answered yes he could see him clearly and he was smiling back.

I told P. to ask the pilot what had happened that day. As far as he knew his plane had crashed but it did not receive enemy fire. P. said he really needed to know if he had overlooked something mechanical that could have caused the crash.

His pilot smiled and said he was fine and in a better place now. And no, P. wasn't at fault. He said it had been his own fault. He had made a dive and strafed the target. Then he pulled up hard into a steep climb and roll. He went into low cloud cover while in the roll and developed vertigo. Before he could recover, he ran into the side of the next hill. P. was quiet and still for a time after that. I could feel his body soften and relax.

He finally gently turned and looked at me. He thanked me for the opportunity to do that. He said it was really important for him to know.

He paused a few minutes longer and then he asked me if I had been in the Vietnam War. I suddenly felt a shift in my body and in my own stillpoint. I told him no I had never been drafted, and, in fact, I had always felt a little guilty about that. When the draft process occurred back then it was a live drawing on T.V. much like today's winning *Megabucks* numbers. When the draft began, we were sent a special number in registered official military mail. My number was 161. Then as the draft began they moved through the calendar day by day. When each day came up, they would pick a card or ball (I can't remember which) with numbers on them. If it was your birthday and they picked your number, you were "volunteered" for Vietnam. On my birthday, May 3, 1951, they picked the card that said 1-160. I missed the draft by one.

I think P. could sense my emotion as I told my little story. He then looked at me, then up at the ceiling and said you know you shouldn't feel guilty about that. All the ones who stayed home protested, and tried to bring him and all the soldiers like him home...they were right—the war was wrong. We should never have been there. We should never have had that war.

I think he felt my body soften and relax and I sensed that he knew I didn't just not go. I protested the war in Washington. Just then, he gave me permission to know that he, a Vietnam Vet, was okay with that. And it was *that permission* that brought an end to my guilt.

I thanked him for MY session and I also thanked him for going to war for me and our country.

As I finish this writing, I am sure we need to be here, now more than ever, with good intended hands and CST. We need to help each other so that we can go on, because as history shows, war goes on. Recent events in the Persian Gulf and the fundamental Muslim extremists now terrorizing the world are leaving deep negative emotions on many peoples of the world. The actions of our own country are leaving current histories of fear, anger, sorrow, grief, and pain at home and abroad. Those that engage the body in a way such as SomatoEmotional Release will be sorely needed to help heal others, and ourselves. As our teacher and mentor John Upledger says, "We need to try and make the world a touch better." Study and practice SER work, and get ready. History is now, and war goes on.

# 29

# Brain Speaks Not? Part I

In the past year I have become fascinated with the possibility and frequent opportunity to dialogue with organs of the brain. Since taking the Brain Speaks class at the UI, I have found occasions when the personalities of inner organs of the head show amazing insights and constructive solutions to health problems for their owner patients.

On many occasions I have thought about where I would be and what I would be doing in my professional life if the Upledger Institute were not part of my continuing education and personal development. I would never have the awareness that there was a palpable body rhythm beyond the cardiac rate and breath. I wouldn't be able to encourage all the forms of physical release for my patients. I would not know about emotions being held in the body. I would not know about energy in the body, energy cysts, vectors, direction of energy, intention. I would not know about Inner Physicians, SomatoEmotional Release or the possibility of dialoging with a portion of the patient's body in order to ascertain the nature of a problem and broker a resolution. And most recently I would never have thought it would be possible to speak to a stem cell, a blood cell, DNA, or the cerebellium. All of this awareness has opened up a whole new world of treatment possibilities that render my days ceaseless adventures. To think that I could be in my third decade of only applying moist heat, massage, and exercises to my PT patients, had it not been for the Upledger Institute, makes me profoundly grateful to the UI.

When one of these highly regarded concepts, such as Brain Speaks awareness, suddenly doesn't work, it's quite a shock and causes me to look for the lesson in it.

I have a wonderful patient teaching me now. She is a medical professional that has suffered from headaches most of her life. She is a mother, wife, and clinician trying to lead an active life and is encumbered by progressively debilitating headaches. Her history includes being hit in the head by a large metal pole that suspended two rubber tire swings between trees when she was 10 years old. She was rendered unconscious and developed a blood clot on the brain that required brain surgery. She has always wondered whether that blow precipitated her lifelong headaches.

She had been in six times for CST and had several releases of the spine, neck, and head, and had a decrease in frequency and intensity of her headaches. But recently they had returned, and she was discouraged and concerned she that would never resolve her problem.

I—in my recent Brain Speaks frame of mind—said to her on her last visit, "Well, maybe we should ask your brain or an organ in your head if that old swing trauma was the source of the problem." I arrogantly thought to myself I could get those organs to confirm that there were lasting results of trauma to the brain and be able to show this mental health professional how real mental health was attained.

With the usual permissions being asked, she thought it might be worth a try. So after I said "And would it be okay if your brain or a part of your brain used your voice mechanism to talk to us?" again she agreed.

So in my confident air I held her by the third vault hold, and opened what I was sure would be fascinating dialogue with her brain.

"Hello Mary's brain, I'm Don. We would sure like to talk to you about Mary's long-term headaches. Maybe you could help us find a solution to her headaches. Will you come forward and talk to me?" Pause...pause...one minute...two minutes go by.

I thought they must be hesitant to speak. They obviously need a little more coaxing to come out, so I reiterated in another way. "I know, brain, that you and all your organs up there are very powerful and wise. I would really be honored if you would come forward and speak to me" Pause...pause...one minute...two minutes, still nothing.

I needed to gently push now. What would she think if I didn't connect? I needed to be more specific, so I continued. "Maybe I should ask each of you separately? Centrium you're the energy antenna at the crown of her head. The bar of the swing struck her on the top of the head. Do you know anything about the swing accident years ago and her current headaches?"

Pause...pause...nothing.

"How about you hippocampus? You remember physical stimulation and information and disseminate it throughout the brain. Do you know about her headaches?"

Pause...pause...again nothing. "Well cerebellium, how about you? You are the ancient part of the brain. You know about motion control, pain, and emotions. You're the old wise one—surely you know about the origin of her headaches?"

Brain speaks not! Maybe I am not as good as I thought I was. Gee, maybe I can't get the brain to speak. I must have left something out in my dialogue. What should I do now? What do I do when the brain doesn't speak? Where do I go? How do I move on from here? What is the patient going to think about this process now?

These questions were streaming through my mind as I held my patient in silence from the occiput. I wondered and thought and, suddenly, something came into my palpatory awareness. I was pulled out of the thought process in my head and thrust into the gentle awareness of the movement in my hands. It was her cranial rhythm, gently, slowly, migrating into and out of my fingers from her occiput. Suddenly, there came a news flash. Hey Don, you can use the rhythm. In my newfound awareness I opened again.

"You know Mary, maybe the brain isn't ready to speak. Would it be okay if I tried to talk to your cranial rhythm?" She said yes, and I continued, "And would it be all right if we set up a yes/no system? I'll ask the questions that can be answered yes or no and we will agree if the answer is yes the cranial rhythm will stop. If the answer is no the rhythm will simply continue uninterrupted. Is that acceptable to you rhythm?" I held my breath…pause…rhythm stopped. 'Oh my, what a relief,' I said to myself, 'thank you rhythm.'

"That's a yes," I said gently in Mary's ear. "It stopped."

"Okay rhythm, thank you very much for agreeing to communicate with us. Do Mary's headaches have something to do with her head injury from the bar of the swing when she was a child?" Rhythm stopped. "That's a yes." "Are the headaches now caused by an injury to part of her brain?" Finally, I thought, an avenue into dialogue with her brain. This will be Brain Speaks at its finest. Pause…rhythm…rhythm…rhythm.

'Oh my god,' I muffled to myself, 'that's a no!' I had another hesitation now. Here I thought we had a fail-safe way of conversing with the brain and now we don't? There's no injury in the brain? 'Now where do I go?' My thought process continued streaming.

That long pause was interrupted by the patient. "It is amazing," she said. "I can hear those answers in my head…I can hear a 'yes' or 'no' an instant before you say what the rhythm did. Where does that come from?"

Suddenly jolted back to the present by her question I thought, 'Yea, where does that come from? Let's ask the rhythm.' "Rhythm, is the cause of her headaches due to some area other than her head?" Pause...pause...rhythm stops. "Yes!" I whispered emphatically. As I looked down on her, I could see her cheeks and lower face and throat were red and flushed. "Hey, your face is flushed," I said.

"Yes I can feel it. It's heat and it goes to my chin, throat, and down the middle of my chest, by my heart."

Suddenly the Brain Speaks class spoke to me. 'Reticular Formation or thymus,' I thought, as I visualized thymus, located just above the heart.

"Rhythm, is there an area or organ outside of the brain that was affected by the swing pole that is causing her headaches?" ...Rhythm stops dead...!!!!!

"Might that blow on the head have affected the thymus rhythm?" Again an abrupt stop, and deep stillness.

Mary spoke, "You know, I can hear the answers in my head. I wonder if this has something to do with my hyperactive thyroid gland and my Hosimoto's Syndrome?" she paused in wonder.

I raced in my head, 'Hosimoto's, that's right, she had mentioned that in an earlier session. That causes problems with heart development and her immune system. Maybe thymus was affected.' I had many more questions than answers now, so we continued.

"Rhythm, did the force of the blow on top of her head from the swing bar compress things in her neck and upper chest?"

"It says, 'Well, yeah,'" Mary voiced, confirming with a smile just as the rhythm came to a stop. "It seems glad you finally got to here," she continued with a slight smile.

"Rhythm," I ventured, "would it be useful to traction her neck from the occiput?"

Rhythm stopped just as Mary said, "With one hand, and then put your other hand here."She physically gently reached up and took one of my hands and placed it on her upper sternum, just to the left of midline. Heat, pulsing, softening, and lengthening followed for several minutes.

After a time it felt very complete and I asked if anything further needed to be done. Rhythm continued uninterrupted.

"When Mary comes again, can we come back and talk to you again Rhythm?" I asked as an avenue toward closure. Rhythm stopped and the patient followed, "It says 'You better!'" She smiled, opened her eyes, and thanked me very much.

Lessons from the sessions are many here. Therapist, be neutral. Don, don't be egotistical and arrogant. Respect the inner guides by honoring them with neutral questions and not prejudgements. Does the Brain speak? Of course it does, but remember it has many voices, of which CS Rhythm is one. You can always count on the rhythm for help. If you stay present, keep listening, blend and trust…good things can happen for the patient—in spite of the therapist.

# 30

# Brain Speaks Not? Part II

*I* thought about my last session with Mary this past week. There were so many things I learned about her, her injury, dialoguing, and myself. My goal in documenting these experiences is to be of assistance and service to you, the reader, and you, the therapist. But as I journal my sessions in this format, I am the student as well.

Mary came in today, one week after the last visit. We talked for several minutes before the session. She said she was fascinated by the last session and really felt it was helpful. She felt a shift in her chest, throat, and head. She was headache-free the whole week, sleeping better and really feeling wonderful, until she woke this morning. For the first time in a week, she felt pressure in her head again. She said it was funny; as soon as she knew what day it was and began to think about coming to this appointment, she could feel pressure in her head.

"Oh," I said facetiously, "Your body must have wanted to give us something to work on today." We both smiled.

"I really believe this is helping me," she offered. "I do, too. Let's see where we go today," I said, ushering her to the table.

She lay down and we began. I started, as I do, at the feet, and moved upward, listening and reacquainting myself with her rhythm. At thoracic inlet I said, "You know, last visit we spoke to thymus and learned that it would be good to return and continue that discussion. Would that be okay with you Mary?"

"Yes!" she said emphatically. She continued with another 'yes' as I asked if it was acceptable that thymus use her voice mechanism to talk to us.

"Hello thymus, its Don."

"Hello," came the return in a soft but authoritative tone.

"Thymus, I remember last visit you had said we could return to talk. I thank you. You also said Mary's injury from the swing bar incident was not in her head, is that right?"

"Yes."

"Tell me thymus, were you injured way back when Mary was injured by the bar falling?"

"Yes." Then there was a pause, followed by, "I've been waiting to talk to someone about it. The neck, throat, and chest were all compressed."

"How can we help you?" I asked.

"I'm not sure!"

"Well, I've learned through my teacher and working with others that sometimes with good intention and direction of energy we can encourage healing cells to be sent out to parts of the body to help other parts heal. I've even heard that many healing immune system cells come from you, thymus."

"Yes, this is true."

"Well thymus, would it be possible if Mary and I put good intention into you from my hands and the rest of her body, so you could move some healing cells from the part of you that is healthy to the part of you that needs healing?"

"Yes, yes, I think this can be done."

Mary said moments later that she felt strange in her sternum. The palm of my hand on her sternum felt as if it was holding a cup of hot coffee. As her body was actively initiating this process I tried to explain.

"Those special stem cells are generated in the marrow-producing portions of the large bones, Mary, in the medullary canals and hollow portions of the bone, along with red and white blood cells. And, thymus, I know how important you are for healing and body defenses. Please accept and transport some of those cells for yourself and heal yourself."

Moments later, Mary had a couple of breath changes and then the distinctive tone of thymus came through Mary's voice, "That feels better, now we need to go to thyroid and then the base of the neck." "Thank you thymus for showing us where to go next. Would it be good to put my fingers on her throat?" I ventured.

"Yes certainly," came the reply.

(I always know I am talking to an authentic Inner Physician when the directions are precise and authoritative. Patients are usually too self-conscious to order the therapist around with such directness.)

Speaking to thymus and Mary, I slowly raised my hands from thoracic inlet and moved superior suddenly stopping at her large thyroid cartilage. "I think I'll hold the thyroid for a moment," I said. The gentle hand of the patient came up from the side and softly moved my anterior hand superior another inch, as Mary said with a giggle—as if she couldn't believe she was moving the therapist's hands again.

"She says you need to open the hyoid first." She giggled again.

"Absolutely," I agreed. (Day 1 CSTI Don!!!) Any thought I'd had of directing the course of this session just evaporated.

"Thank you thymus. I feel like we need to send stem cells to thyroid, hyoid, the cervical spine."

"Yes we will, I'll tell you when to move to each," came thymus admonishingly.

We stayed here for what seemed like ten minutes, then, I felt a slight shift as if I were standing in the current of a river and it suddenly changed as if someone had stopped ahead of me up stream. The energy and flow stopped. I took it as a repelling sign that we were finished here and needed to move on.

"Now we should go to thyroid," thymus directed, "there is a different type of injury there."

I suddenly thought she must be talking about the Hoshimoto's Syndrome Mary was diagnosed with shortly after her swing accident.

Then Mary's own voice came in, "I'm getting the thought and the word repeated in my head...airway...." My mind was racing now. Airway, what did that mean? Does she have a lung problem? Did her old injury affect her bronchial tree or her trachea? My mouth opened and asked before I knew it, "Thymus was her thyroid injured during the swing mishap years ago?"

Mary came in again, "She says yes, but is hesitant, its not the same, it's different."

I asked more questions, kind of thinking out loud, "Did the injury to thyroid happen during the swing accident?"

"Not long after."

I remembered Mary saying she had to have brain surgery to relieve a blood clot on the crown of her head. Could this have been part of the surgery, I thought to myself.

"She says yes," Mary volunteered, then smiled. "She heard your question to yourself and the answer is yes."

"I never cease to be amazed at the dialoging process. When you are in the thick of it, there is thought entrainment.

"Thymus you are so amazing and powerful. Tell me, are you able to see the whole body on the inside? Is that how you know so much?"

"I can see and feel everything that happens to this body."

I suddenly felt a deep sense of trust coming from this body and this Inner Physician. We were coming from that place of trust and moving to a new level.

"Thymus, was the thyroid injured as she was intubated and the airway tube inserted in her throat for anesthesia for her brain surgery after the swing accident?"

"Yes," came the answer followed by a long stillness. I felt as if the thymus was quiet with sadness, and Mary was quiet with the sudden awareness of a traumatic piece of her history just now being revealed to her for the first time.

"I wish to send cells here now," thymus interjected. We passed more quiet time until again I felt a soft but sudden surge of energy change in my fingers that had held thyroid.

Mary then began to have gentle regional tissue releases from the neck, and her head began to gently turn side to side.

Seeking new instruction I said, "Thymus would it be helpful to have my fingers at the base of the head, maybe doing a little gentle traction?"

"Yes, that would be very good, the muscles and joints need to stretch."

I assumed the Occipital Cranial Base position and moved quickly through platform, gapping C-1 and spreading the condyles, so I could begin a slow dural tube traction from occiput. We deviated to the left and right a couple of times, pausing in a flexion movement with the head and neck.

"Is there any more work to be done here today, Thymus?" I asked, sensing an end to the session.

"No, that's all for now. This has been very good. Be sure to put this in your book!"

"Okay," like I needed one more surprise. I smiled in pleasant disbelief, "Thank you very much thymus!"

As I sat back on my stool and Mary sat up she said she never thought anything like this was possible. "I know I'm going to be well again."

"Mary, did I tell you I was writing a book? I told you didn't I?"

"Yes, I think you mentioned it last visit when you asked if you could document the last session." "She smiled, knowing the sudden relief on my face was the realization that her Inner Guide and Physician was not the all-knowing creature I thought she was from that last comment about the book. I think all three of us smiled inside.

Lessons from the Session: The Brain Speaks. Inner knowing is accessible and an important catalyst for facilitating healing and change. Some of you therapists may be like this therapist and need constant reminders to trust the process. Trust what you hear for advice, and do what you are told. Patient results will be better. Your life will flow better.

# 31

# The Study Group Tree

We have been holding study groups at my office in Rochester. for several years. I was fortunate enough to buy an old dairy farm with a farmhouse, creamery, barn, and large garage. The owner was a former patient of mine and we became close friends. Together we developed the farmhouse into my office and created a large circular driveway. It circled around an island with a large beautiful maple tree and a huge stone well cap. He told me about the tree. It had been planted some 50 years ago in memory of his friend's son who had been killed in a plane crash. When I bought the place he asked me not to cut it. I told him I loved it too and promised to keep it as long as I could.

Well, Bill died in 1994 and I tried my best to care for his tree. It began experiencing poor leaf out about five years ago. I put nutrition spikes in the ground to no avail. Each year, large central limbs died and broke off, landing in the driveway and parking area. I finally felt I had to cut it down and last weekend did indeed do that. I cut all burnable wood to fireplace length and hauled it home. During a recent study group, while waiting for my students to arrive, I became a bit melancholy. I was gazing out from the office kitchen window at the empty circle and the remnants of that old tree.

As students came, (three in all) each asked what happened to the tree. In casual conversation before meeting, I told them the story.

I usually start by asking whoever shows up what they want to talk about. One said she wanted to go over the 10-Step hand placements. Another wanted me to talk about how you get someone to have a SomatoEmotional Release. And the third wanted to know how to hold a space for a person to have an SER without becoming emotional herself. I thought about it and began by having the 10-Step review student begin a 10-Step on the student wanting to know about SER. The holding space student and I would comment as the practice unfolded.

Unfold it did. From respiratory Diaphragm the patient went into a still point. Her hands went out to her sides, then up over her head. I asked her what she was feeling. She said she was thinking about the tree outside that was recently cut down. The stump and about 10 feet of the thick trunk of the tree remained lying on the ground. It was more than I could cut up in one weekend. She said she couldn't stop thinking about the boy who had died and now the tree had died, too. It made her think of death and her planned trip the next weekend to see her dying father. She said she didn't know if her father was ready to die. Her family didn't talk about those things.

I asked her to picture her father and then I asked her to ask him how he felt about death. She asked and readily heard and saw his response in her mind's eye. He said he was scared, and sad he hadn't been the best of fathers. She began to cry and felt like she wanted to be curled up and held by him.

Then her sister came into the picture. She had died over nine years ago. I asked her why she thought her sister had come by. Through tears (she and her sister were very close) and long pauses, she learned her sister had come by to help their dad get to the other side.

By this time I was at her feet and the holding space student was doing just that, holding space from a vault hold of the patient's head. The holding space student got a little emotional, then regrouped and stayed right there. The patient watched (as did we all in our mind's eye) as her sister merged with the energy of their father and both began to glow brightly. Several minutes passed when I asked how things were going. The patient said, "Wonderful." The three of them had been joined together in a warm glowing place that was peaceful and comforting to all. Her father wasn't afraid anymore. She was now looking forward to her trip in the coming weekend.

She opened her eyes and thanked each of us in turn. When she came to me, I asked her if she had any more questions about SER?? We all laughed. But suddenly, it dawned on us that we all got our needs met. She experienced an SER and learned about dialogue that helped move her in and out of her session. The 10-Step student did some of that, got a still-point and witnessed what was possible. And the holding space student got a little emotional with her patient but was able to energetically pull back just enough to stay connected with the session and enough to hold space without adding her own emotional release to the session.

I, too, was able to see that there was an added dimension to life in my cutting down the old tree. It was the fallen tree that triggered the SER student to contemplate death and move into the needed release of the emotional charge of her father's imminent transition. I mean, how many trees in the forest can say they had an impact on human consciousness, as this tree had? This gave all of us elements of what we needed. I was glad and honored for the extra meaning and nature's connection to our lives that unfolded from my old tree.

The lesson from this session is that there is consciousness that is connected and naturally all around us. We can learn about life if we are willing to look and listen. This group of people was served and their consciousness raised by this natural living thing's experience of death. The study of CST in small group format is very meaningful for experiential growth. Each study group plants seeds for the future.

# Part V

## Lessons in the End

# 32

# The Amazing Grace of Farewell

When we come to the events of great loss in our life, we suffer. We experience elements of fear, anger, denial, negotiation, and acceptance.* Along the way are a myriad of feelings—physical and emotional. Sometimes the feelings are brief and very forgettable like, "Darn, we lost the game 'cause I struck out." At other times loss is profound, like, "I'm sorry to tell you this, but he/she has died," or "I wish there was something we could do but he/she/you are terminally ill." Bad words are energy cyst bullets.

As Ram Dass says. "We take our personalites as real." Death is very traumatic for the personality, because if you don't have a body, personality has nothing to do and no longer exists. Terminality means the quality of coming to an end, bringing to a close, occurring each term. Termination is serious business for the subject. It means transition and change are imminent. In the forest, ants run for cover when their anthill is stepped on. Deer and rabbits run for their lives when threatened by hunters. Squirrels all know roads are dangerous. Even the flower fains for light rather than darkness and grows toward the sun.

Death, loss, and termination are all forms of goodbye. Goodbye is a contracted word form of "God be with You." Goodbye is farewell: a leave taking, a last parting, an admonition to travel on, and fare well. When one fares well, one is able to manage, get

---

* Elisabeth Kübler-Ross

along, experience luck, and have ample food and supplies for the journey. When we talk about wellness and provide service in healthcare, as providers, we can be of great service to people in the active process of dying. We can aid them in faring well.

In the process of death, each of us will experience the greatest goodbye. It is the culminating event of our personal time here. It is a loss so profound for our physical body that cultures are built around understanding, denying, and fighting it. It is the most significant threat to our personality each of us can ever experience.

I mean here we are, vital and healthy—mobile, active, functional—experiencing life with our senses. A name and persona is given to each of us in this lifetime. Then we experience physical or mental loss and one or more of our senses doesn't work. Our mobility is reduced. Contentment and happiness are replaced by sadness, fear, and pain. Our physical world begins to reduce to our home. As losses continue we move to one room, then a bed. We must in whatever process it takes, give back our bodies . We are no longer who we once were. We give up the use of our legs, arms, eyes, ears, taste, smell, and touch. Finally, our world is reduced to being in our head. Slowly breath stops, the heart stops, and we are left with the final transitional moments of our stream of life (CranioSacral Rhythm or Cranial Rhythmic Impulse). Our ceaseless wave ceases and draws to a final still point and the original energy returns to consciousness. The rest is a mystery but I believe the last elements of Cranial Rhythmic Impulse energy is enough to fare us well into the great beyond. In India, when someone dies, the pronouncement of death is defined as "dropping the body." What an acknowledgment that we go on!

With all this in mind I have learned lessons from being allowed to be witness to transitions of lifetimes, including my own.

Some of the words said and other happenstances of my family member's transition are private and sacred and not published here. But some of the natural grace that occurs with death is universal and beautiful and should be shared. There are some life moments that will happen to everybody. To move the unknown into the known is the greatest way I know to remove fear. I honor my ancestors' lives as vehicles for change, understanding, and the abolishment of fear. I share with you now, so in the event you are asked to be present for someone's major transition and farewell you will have had at least this experience.

My grandmother died in her 93rd year. She died in the house she had lived in for over 50 years. Living to be so old she had years to sit by herself and contemplate her transition. She used to tell us she was waiting to go. It would make us all smile and always bring any family gathering discussion of death nicely to a change of subject space.

It took her years to leave her body. She lived for weeks at a time with my mother and father, then she would return for a time to her little house. My uncle lived in the next town. Nana lived in a white cape on a corner lot of a little dead-end street in Riverside, and my uncle lived in Old Greenwich. He would cut her lawn and other handyman activities, as well as visit her daily. Finally the travel to and from my parents' house became too much and my mother spent a week at a time with Nana in the old house in Riverside. We hired home nursing to come help, and Nana went from her house, to her room, to her bed. Finally, bedridden, my mom, uncle, and I took turns staying at her side. Her days and nights blended in endless swings of consciousness and sleep. We held the straw so she could sip water or a spoon for a taste of pudding. We gave her a moist washcloth or rubbed her legs or just held her hand. Mom and the nurse would help with private chores.

Her last night was one of restless slips in and out of sleep. I remember being alone with her. It was 3:00 am. Suddenly there was an alertness to her and she sat up in bed and said she could see them all waiting for her. I asked who, and she recited the names of all her brothers and sisters and parents, who had gone before. Her child who had died not long after birth was there as well. She was a little troubled as she continued speaking because she didn't know how to get there. Her rhythm was in still point. I told her she could just close her eyes and look for them with her eyes closed. When she saw them she could just move forward toward them in her mind.

My mom, sleeping in another room, heard the conversation and our movements as Nana tried to sit up. At one point she tried to get out of bed. Mom heard this and came in. Being an R.N., she took Nana's pulse, found it was racing, and called my uncle. He and his wife quickly dressed and arrived within 20 minutes or so. I had remained at the far side of the bed, holding Nana's hand and monitoring her rhythm, which had been still but now had returned.

With all of us around her bedside, I relayed to all the conversation we had. Each in turn said to Nana that we were there and it was okay to go...we just sat in quiet witness. The night, the room, the small bedstand light—all the people gathered—were physically still, but energetically we were all one and formed a circle of loving, hopeful, peaceful, intent. We then became aware of the weakening of her breath. Before, her body had been anxious and she was visibly breathing heavy, but now it had slowed and softened to an irregular faint puff. Pauses became longer, maybe 30–40 seconds, until one pause just continued. I was then aware of her heart rate. It too wained away and was gone. Then I was in a space of pure mystery. I was now listening to a body (the beloved body of my Nana) that didn't breath and didn't have a heartbeat. But there was a gentle tide that was silently, rhythmically, energetically producing a wave through this body, whose soul was rising. As I watched with my hands, the little waves that slide up on the sandy beach just became smaller. The frequency was unchanged, just the volume diminished until there was nothing.

I waited and searched my senses for other signs of life. This pause seemed like the end. All motion had ceased. All life surely was vacated. I looked at my mother, aunt, and uncle. There was a sense that it was over.

To our surprise, Nana's body gave up one more gasp, as if awakened suddenly. Then a greater stillness, the depth of which I had never known. We all knew she was gone. She had dropped her body. As I write this, it seems to me the original energy spark that had begun this life nearly a century ago, somehow reached a final threshold, enough to eject the consciousness of this body out and away. My Nana was home and in the arms of loved ones.

It seemed like only a short time later, but it was a matter of years when my Mom began closing down her physicality. She had been a lifelong smoker. It seemed like everybody in medicine and healthcare in the sixties and seventies smoked. She was a fantastic mother, grandmother, and nurse. She had returned to nursing after raising her family, as a way of overcoming the empty nest syndrome of middle age. She then cared for her mother until she passed, and then talked Dad into selling their large house in the Philadelphia suburbs for something smaller. They sold their home and moved into a multi-level senior citizen's living complex. She had wanted to move into Nana's old house but it was decided Nana's house was to be sold shortly after she passed. After it was sold it was promptly torn down. A new modern multimillion dollar ultra modern living unit took its place. It is now owned by a New York City commuter, who walks to the train station every day. We all experienced a big goodbye in the loss of our childhood family home when Nana's house was gone. Goodbye requires letting go.

So Mom and Dad settled in this senior citizen's deal in which they had a two bedroom, one story condo-style home in a gated community. Couples who could move about on their own could live in a villa. It had a small yard and a double carport, adjoined to the next villa. All homes were on little dead-end streets, nicely landscaped with shrubs and sidewalks. There was trolley service to the central senior center. The center had dining, theater, bar, library, church services, special events, outdoor pool, and the whole complex was connected to several levels of skilled nursing care. As one lost function there would be a level of care to ensure each resident would fare well for life.

As it happened Mom was in a wheelchair, on oxygen, and really struggling when they moved into the villa. She lasted there for three months before difficulty with breathing, generalized weakness, and respiratory infection brought her to the skilled nursing unit. A fall in the bathroom there, and her world narrowed rapidly from home to room and then constant nursing care. Progressive weakness, weight and appetite loss, and decreasing active movement of arms and legs brought her to the confines of her bed. She had loved to sit in her chair in her old home, watching the birds at the feeder. She had missed the birds that spring. It was mid summer and we were in the middle of a drought, so the heat and dryness had kept her inside in the air conditioning. So by that point in the year she had said goodbye to her old home, her old life, and her physical independence—and the birds.

The family seemed to be unified in wanting to stay close to Mom and understanding that she was getting ready to leave. There is nothing that brings a family together more than deathwatch. You sit across the bed looking at each other and take breaks for quiet talks about really meaningful things. When one sits quietly with someone in the process of dying, all your extraneous bullshit melts away. Thoughts are not of yourself, but of how you can be present and be a good listener for the all-important person in the transition process. The patient knows; there is quiet acceptance that descends on all that are present. Sometimes struggle makes acceptance a distant goal for the person in process and family members. Sometimes letting go is hard.

As we sat there with her, I recall, like Nana, I was holding her hand and arm. My sister and brother and father were there. And my uncle, Mom's brother, was there by her side. We each said we loved her and she could do whatever she needed to do. If she wanted to stay, we would stay with her. If she wanted to go, we would miss her, but we wanted her to know all would be okay, and Nan and Pop and the whole family would meet her on the other side.

Again I recalled the body changing. We all made a human energy circle, just concentrating on encouraging Mom to do what she needed to do. And again her breath quieted slowly, then stopped. Deeper down, her cardiac rate trailed off, and, once again, I felt a deep gentle wave of rhythm with a constant rate, but slowly, over a minute or two, the volume just faded away to nothing. Another 30–60 seconds passed and again this beautiful body rendered up a burst of energy and a quick gasp that startled us. Instant terminality dawned on us all.

I was moved by some urge to go to the window and open it. I remember so well the following events. It was late afternoon and none of us had noticed, but it had been raining, as all the foliage was shimmering and dripping. As I returned to Mom's side I got a sense that a wave of energy was streaming up and out of her. We were witnessing her dropping her body. It went to the ceiling and circled all around the bed in a gentle swirl as if someone had suddenly opened a door to the outside. The gentle comforting swirl continued around us—giving us a final farewell—and then gently away, past the bed by the window , which was empty, and on out the window. I was struck by this energy sense and brought back to the physical plane by the afternoon setting sunlight streaming through the open window and the sound of birds in the trees just outside. Our tears of sorrow were washed away by such natural unifying confirmation that the natural spirit had just embraced my mom and she was free to fly like her beloved birds and breath as the breeze after a summer shower. This was such natural grace. I was so grateful and honored to know Mom was a part of this beautiful transformation. I can never be dissuaded from the thought that we are all universal force and consciousness, and simply change form at the end of our term.

There is no greater recognition of what is important in life until one's own life continuance is called into question. The reality of death is that everyone will be successful at it. And as much as we think we know, no one knows exactly when and exactly how their death will occur. Neither do medical experts.

I went to get a physical years ago. It was required in order to be a hospice volunteer at a local home nursing agency. The doctor was a friend and knew me and my practice as a physical therapist, doing CranioSacral Therapy. He asked me if I ever came in contact with fluids. I told him patients sometimes cry during SomatoEmotional Release and I do go in the mouth frequently to access cranial bones at the roof of the mouth and floor of the cranial vault. I added that I had contact with oral fluids but have my hands fully gloved.

He followed that AIDS is an issue with healthcare personnel and body fluids, and for the safety of my family, I should really be tested. Since he put it that way, I agreed.

When being tested for AIDS you must register with the center for disease control in Atlanta. You must be tested (have your blood drawn) by a certified AIDS testing phlebotomist. You must fill out special forms and go into a separate room away from other blood drawing stations. Results come under different cover and directly to your physician. Turn-around time then (mid 1990's) was 2–3 weeks.

A few weeks later I received my routine blood work results in the mail from my doctor's office. A note on the lab report stated that the results of the AIDS test would come under separate cover. I waited and it didn't come. I waited and I waited—three weeks, four weeks, five weeks. As life does, it opened up for me a unique opportunity to experience fear and paranoia, which made me less and less able to be brave enough to call my doctor for the results.

I thought secretly and continuously. Bill got the results but he doesn't want to tell me. Yup, I've got AIDS and the Center for Disease Control in Atlanta is making arrangements now to close my practice. I am going to lose my practice and lose my house. Then I will lose my life. What will happen to the kids, and Jill. AIDS drugs cost a fortune. My insurance won't pay for them. I'll either waste away in a hospital bed alone or in front of my family at home. They'll have to take care of me and watch me die. I am too young for this. I don't deserve this. I didn't do any of the things people do to get AIDS. How could this happen to me?

I became very quiet. I was unable to sleep and was very silent at the table and in the car with the family. I began to speak very softly and agreed with my kids and my wife on everything. I began following my wife around and asking to help plant shrubs and weed the gardens with her. I refused to make love. I had an intense need not to be alone. Then there were times when I had to be alone. The most intense sadness came over me at different times. The waves of sadness and not knowing what to do arose in me with such intensity I had all I could do to sit and continue to breath. Sometimes in the car driving alone, I would just start to cry. If slow instrumental music came on the radio I would feel melancholy and mournful. Some days I would be going along okay and suddenly I couldn't function and another wave of sadness and fear covered me like a heavy net.

I wasn't doing good physical therapy then. Fortunately, a lot of my practice was still routine modality delivery. I could simply deliver moist heat, ultrasound, massage, and exercise with brief social pleasantries. I wasn't being a particularly good listener because I couldn't stay present for my patients.

Six weeks went by. Seven weeks, then eight weeks go by. I still hadn't told anyone. I couldn't tell Jill. I couldn't have her experience this awful feeling of fear and despair. There was nothing to do but wait to get sick and to have my world fall apart. My worry, fear, anxiety, and sleeplessness began to cause me to lose weight, which only confirmed to me the fact that I had full-blown AIDS and my immune system was auto digesting. I looked all over my body for signs of skin lesions. I had been doing my own CV4 and self releasing of my constantly torsioning sphenoid by holding both greater wings of sphenoid with one hand and my other hand in my mouth, thumb-sucking vomer and ethmoid into mobilizing.

Waves upon waves of heavy grief and fear came and went. I couldn't talk to anyone I cared for about this because I didn't want them to feel what I was feeling. Finally, I couldn't bear it, I had to know. I had to turn myself in and move into the logistics of disassembling my life. So I went upstairs to my private office and closed the door. I called my doctor but he wasn't available. I left a message and I waited for him to call back. I said I hadn't heard about my AIDS test results and I really needed to know! (It was a much bigger question then it sounded. I mean I was waiting like I was waiting when I asked my wife to marry me.)

"Oh Don, gee, didn't my secretary call you? Gee, that was weeks ago. The results were fine, gee I hope it didn't cause you any undue concern."

I said, "Oh, no; that's okay, that's okay, I just needed to know…thanks a lot….gotta run…have a great day." I hung up, thinking to myself, I now know how it feels to be terminal.

The lesson in it for me is that I have since been able to be present for patients who are dying. I can ask them about how they feel. I can notice their far away look when a wave of fear, sadness, or despair comes. I can put my hands on them and give them a stillpoint and then sit with them with the intention of being present. Listening to the rhythm as they enter transition, and their inner bodies move into grace, I can stay there and be a witness and wish them farewell. Sometimes great healing takes place as someone comes to acceptance of the place they are in, within the circle of their life. A goal of working with the dying is to help them understand their life events. Helping them to become aware of their inner voice is a great step toward helping them to fare well on their great journey from this lifetime into the beyond.

Lessons from these sessions are that grace is all around. This life is so connected by a universal consciousness and energy that grace is the nearest word that fits. Grace is intense, powerful, awesome, and awful. It is the moments when life's meanings become clear. It is accessed by coming to stillness. CST can help bring a person or a group of people to stillness—enough to come to grace—and can aid the traveler on their journey.

For all readers, especially practitioners, may this not come as a surprise, but you are dying. The more you practice stillpoints, going inward, listening and being present, the more you will help fellow human beings in transition, and the more practice you will have for your own transition. You can learn to be an aid to others and your own welfare. So farewell.

# 33

# The Lesson of Intention

When I decided to write this book, it was because of a desire to express what I have learned over many years of doing CST. But it would be incomplete if I did not include what I observed and learned in going to and coming from my place of work and the sessions.

If I put into one word what is important in life—in conscious living, and in working with people towards health and wellness—it is: Intention. CST is intentional touch.

Defined by Webster *intention* is "a determination to act in a specific way, anything intended. *Intend* is "to plan, purpose, to mean to be or used for." *Taber's Medical Dictionary* defines *intention* as (Latin *in*, upon, and *tendere* to stretch) "[1]A natural process of healing. [2]Goal or purpose." Our goal and purpose in CST is to touch, listen to the body, and have the intention to remain impartial, non judgmental, ego subordinate, and unconditionally present.

What I have learned is that intention is a thread that weaves itself throughout the fabric of life. The magnificent sunflower commonly grows eight to 10 feet and has a flower and seed-pod of thousands of seeds and weighing several pounds. The stalk is often as thick as a human wrist. The giant plant turns each day and places the face of its seedpod directly toward the path of the sun. It faces east in the morning and west at sunset. All this because a seed, weighing less than five grams, had the intention to initiate the spark of life and become a great plant.

211

I was driving to my session one day in the fall. As I came over a hill I slowed my old truck down, as there was some kind of animal in the road. I looked and looked at what was the strangest animal I had ever seen. It seemed to be a large squirrel but it was stretched out, and irregular shaped. And it was moving. As I got closer I came to a full stop. There before me was one squirrel carrying another injured squirrel off the road. Here was intention. Here was a high order of purpose. Here was selflessness personified. Here was bravery and kindness. Here was a natural process of healing, in that someone had the intent to try to bring another to a point of safety and out of harm's way. This was a purposeful act, usually attributed to firemen, police officers and healthcare workers.

I was once asked to lecture to the staff of the Boston Aquarium on body mechanics and lifting. The young marine biologists and scientists were injuring their backs loading the thousands of pounds of boxed frozen fish required weekly to feed the Dolphins, Sea Lions, and seals.

I had invited my daughter to spend the day with me. The staff gave us a guided tour through the facility and took us under the bleachers to the backside of the show pool, not viewed by the public. Using a whistle they called in the dolphins and allowed my daughter and me to pet the large wondrous animals.

I'll never forget the largest one. When the trainers used their whistle he came and took a fish and then swam away. Moments after, my daughter and I went to the platform. He swam by us, maybe ten to twelve feet away. But it was like he was a kayak moving effortlessly in the slightest current of a quiet water stream. He moved maybe one foot every two or three seconds so that it seemed like a full minute for him to go by us. And he was listing to one side so that his large right eye was out of the water looking at us. I should say he was looking into us. I felt a sense of self-consciousness and a strange feeling of being examined. I felt a narrow gentle band of some kind of energetic wave move down me from my head to the middle of my calf. My daughter said he made her feel "funny" too. I had a sudden itch in my stomach area and began to scratch. In retrospect I wonder if it had anything to do with my gallbladder that eventually had to be removed. He then came to the side of the pool and allowed us to stroke him. I felt there was some kind of intention from him that day.

Dolphins are amazing creatures. They are soft to the touch; the skin is like velvet. But underneath they are dense, solid, and very powerful. They are able to swim ahead of a ship traveling 30 knots and faster. They can easily weigh 300 to 600 pounds, and are known to repel sharks with a torpedo like punch from their blunt nose. (Rostrum)

A story that has come out of Florida, but unrelated to Upledger work, also has to do with dolphins. It seems there was an aquarium that had a "swim with the dolphins" experience for the public. For a fee you were allowed to swim with the dolphins, accompanied by trainers. It was an outside area of fenced-in shoreline that was part of the aquarium. Everyone was in the water having a beautiful dolphin experience, when a very startling event occurred. A tall middle-aged woman was in the water just a few yards from the rest of the group. The great animals were gently swimming among the rest of the people. All of a sudden, one of the larger dolphins swam up to the woman and presented itself only two or three feet directly in front of her. The huge animal then moved forward and landed its blunt, shark-repeller nose right in the middle of this lady's chest, so that she gasped, grabbed her chest, and fell backwards in the water and went under.

The trainers rushed to her and pulled her up and ushered her dockside. She had shortness of breath and a look of horror on her face. Others were in a state of panic, moving as rapidly as they could to help her and also to remove themselves from the water. Dry land did not remove her anxiety, pain, or fear of injury, so they transported her to the hospital where she was examined and x-rayed, and then moved to the operating room for emergency surgery. They discovered she had a large tumor growing on the wall of her aorta. Had it not been identified and removed it would surely have breeched the wall of the great artery and been fatal. It was exactly and directly beneath the right edge of the lower sternum and precisely where the dolphin had struck her with his nose.

Some may call this coincidence. Some may say it was impossible for the dolphin to have known about the tumor. I believe that this was/is intention of the highest order. I believe that at great risk and personal sacrifice, this benevolent creature attempted to solicit medical attention for someone of another species. This dolphin is a veterinarian.

The great lesson from these life sessions is Intention. It is what makes a session a treatment and not a protocol. It is the power of placebo and beyond. It is the ignition of the power of self-healing. It is the spark of life. It is the confounding dilemma of double blind study. It is the reason the public is turning toward integrative medicine. It is the underlying current of truth. It is the nature of good and evil, fear and love. It is the ultimate Lesson from the Sessions, and is to be explored as a fundamental goal of this lifetime. I wish you a great adventure and a happy life.

# 34

## The Lesson of It

*"It"* is the work known as CranioSacral Therapy.
The work is the transfer of force
from one body to another.

The force is 5 grams of intentional manual
pressure applied to the CranioSacral Rhythm.

To do it, means to feel it.

To feel it, means to know it.

To know it, means to learn it.

To learn it, means to study it.

Once you know it, you always feel it.

The lesson of "It" is:
Once you always feel it, you can forget
about it, and just put your hands on
the person with good intention, no judgment,
and hold space for healthy change.

There, you have It!

# Bibliography

Adams, P. (1993) *Gesundheit*. Vermont: Healing Arts Press

Arbuckle, B. (undated) *The Select Writings of Beryl Arbuckle*. Ohio: American Academy of Osteopathy

Alvord, L. (1999) *The Scalpel and the Silver Bear*. New York: Bantam Books

Aristotle, (1943) *On Man in the Universe*. New York: Walter J. Black Inc.

Calais-Germain, B. (1993) *Anatomy of Movement*. Washington: Eastland Press

Castaneda, C. (1969) *The Teachings of Don Juan*. California : University of California Press

Chopra, D. (1993) *Ageless Body, Timeless Mind*. New York: Harmony Books

Chopra, D. (1989) *Quantum Healing*. New York: Bantam Books.

Cohen, B. B. (1993) *Sensing Feeling and Action*. Mass: Contact Editions

Cohen, K. (1997) *The Way of Qigong*. New York: Ballantine Books.

Cousins, N. (1979) *Anatomy of an Illness*. New York: Bantam Books.

Dalai Lama, The (2001) *An Open Heart*. Mass, New York, England: Little Brown and Company

Dass, R, (1976) *Grist for the Mill*. California: Celestial Arts

Frankl, V. (1959) *Man's Search for Meaning*. Mass: Beacon Press

Grof, S. & Bennett, H. (1993) *Holotropic Mind*. New York: Harper Collins Publishing

Hunt, V. (1989) *Infinite Mind*. California: Malibu Publishing Co.

Jung, CG. (1961) *Memories, Dreams, Reflections*. Canada: Random House Inc.

Julian, D. (1987) *Job's Body, A Handbook for Bodywork*. New York: Station Hill Press, Inc.

Kaptchuk, T. (1983) *The Web That Has No Weaver*. New York: Congdon & Weed Inc.

Levine, P. (1997) *Walking the Tiger: Healing Trauma*. California: North Atlantic Books

Levine, S. (1987) *Healing into Life and Death*. New York: Doubleday

Mails, T. (1991) *Fools Crow, Wisdom and Power*. Oklahoma: Council Oak Books

McTaggart, L. (2002) *The Field*. New York: Harper Collins

Milne, H. (1995) *The Heart of Listening*. California: North Atlantic Books

Monte, T. (1993) *The East West Guide to Healing Your Body*. New York: Putnam Publishing Group

Oschman, J. (2000) *Energy Medicine, The Scientific Basis*. England: Churchill Livingstone

Perls, F. (1969) *Gestalt Therapy Verbatim*. New York: Bantam Books

Pert, C. (1997) *Molecules of Emotion*. New York: Scribner

Seton, E. & J. (1966) *The Gospel of the Redman*. New Mexico: Seton Village

Smith, F.F. (1986) *Inner Bridges*. Georgia: Humanics New Age.

Siegel, B. (1993) *Love, Medicine & Miracles*. New York: Harper & Row Publishing Inc.

Sutherland, W. G. (1971) *Contributions of Thought*. Rudra Press

Upledger, J., Vredevoogd, J., (1983) *CranioSacral Therapy*. Washington: Eastland Press

Upledger, J. (1990) *SomatoEmotional Release and Beyond*. Florida: UI Publishing

Upledger, J. (1996) *A Brain is Born*. California: North Atlantic Books.

Upledger, J. (2002) *SomatoEmotional Release – Deciphering the Language of Life*. California: North Atlantic Books

Upledger, J. (2003) *Cell Talk*. California: North Atlantic Books.

Valentine, T.& C. Hetrick, D. (1985) *Applied Kinesiology*. Vermont: Healing Arts Press

Vishnudevananda, S. (1960) *The Complete Illustrated Book of Yoga*. New York: Bell Publishing

Watts, A. (1975) TAO *The Watercourse Way*. New York:
Random House

Williamson, M. (1994) *Illuminata:*. California:
Malibu Publishing Co.

Wilson, C. (1966) *The New Existentialism*. Illinois: Whitehall Co.

# About the Author

*D*on Ash is a physical therapist. He lives with his wife on a farm in rural seacoast New Hampshire.

He has an undergraduate degree in Psychology from Huron University, Huron, South Dakota, and a certificate degree in Physical Therapy from the University of Pennsylvania. He is Diplomate Certified in CranioSacral Therapy from the Upledger Institute, for which he teaches and lectures internationally.

You can contact Don with comments about this book or to obtain his audio recording called *Breath Venting* by writing to him:

Don Ash
Alliance Physical Therapy
243 Rochester Hill Rd.
Rochester, NH 03867

TEL: 603-332-1881
WEB: www.DonAshPT.com